Henk Bruggeman

Living in
Sonship

Revelation from
the Father heart of God

malcolm down

PUBLISHING

Copyright © 2020 Henk Bruggeman

First published 2017 by Great Life Publishing, Westervoort, Netherlands
This book was originally published in Dutch with the title:
'Leven vanuit Zoonschap'

24 23 22 21 20   7 6 5 4 3 2 1

British Library Cataloguing in Publication Data
A catalogue record for this book is available from the British Library.

ISBN 978-1-912863-41-9

NOTE: The bold emphases in Bible quotations are author's own.

Cover design by Esther Kotecha
Art direction by Sarah Grace

Printed in the UK

More information on books and CDs recommended by the
author in this book, as well as the books and CDs themselves,
are available at www.fatherhouse.movement.com

Endorsements

Living in Sonship is a deep and real journey into the heart of the Father that will certainly transform the life of anyone who reads it. Henk's life is a tribute to this reality. He has dedicated his ministry to make this powerful message known throughout the world. As a result, he has helped many make the journey from orphans to sons and daughters of our perfect Father. The fruit of his life and ministry speaks for itself and we know that it will do the same for all who read this book.

Ivan and Isabel Allum
Senior pastors of Forest City Destiny Church
Itinerant speakers

I have been honoured to know Henk for several years. We have ministered together on many occasions, spent time together and shared with others what we have learned about the Father. We have been living a parallel journey, encountering the love of the Father, being radically transformed by it, and then ministering from it, to bring people, by the Holy Spirit, into their sonship. I love Henk's deep passion and commitment to bring this revelation to many needy people, internationally. I admire his heart and value what he has to say and have seen wonderful fruit from his ministering through his Fatherhouse Ministry.

Ian Ross
Father Heart Ministry, Canada

I have thoroughly enjoyed reading this book. Wow, Henk really knows what he's talking about! It's not just theoretical knowledge conceived in a study, but experiential knowledge that's been wrestled out with the Father Himself in the highs and lows of his own life. The revelation in this book come directly out of the Father heart of God. Henk's humour and self-reflection make this book a very enjoyable read. At the end of each chapter he helps you to further reflect, by writing out some things or listening to a song. This provides a deeper experience and makes things very practical. What impacted me the most, is what the Amplified Bible states in Ephesians 3:17-19: '[that you may come] to know [practically, through personal experience] the love of Christ which far surpasses [mere] knowledge [without experience]'. That is my prayer for the whole Netherlands. That everyone will personally start to experience this love!

Johan den Hartogh
Justice House of Prayer (JHOP), Den Haag

Living in Sonship is a book that takes you on a journey into the Father heart of God. Henk frequently speaks at Youth With A Mission on the Father heart of God. His message forms a channel for God's love to touch the hearts of young people. Just like Floyd McClung's book *The Father Heart of God*, this book will help you discover how to let go of the orphan mentality, which so often still ensnares us, and instead, enter into the life of a beloved son or daughter. God's love for us in unconditional. Henk's own journey into sonship is a living example of the reality that we can experience God's tangible presence and peace, right in the middle of the storms of life. This results in a transformation of the heart, which is very much needed in the world today.

Steve Smith
Youth With a Mission, Alblasserwaard

Henk has been speaking for over fifteen years on the revelation of the Father heart of God, in the Netherlands and abroad. As a good friend and brother, I have always enjoyed his passion, humour, insight and most importantly, his closeness with the One whom Jesus came to reveal . . . Our Father in heaven. As Jesus says: 'Now this is eternal life: that they know you, the only true God, and Jesus Christ, whom you have sent' (John 17:3). I pray, and believe, that through this book you will find the Father.

John Nuttall
Worship leader, speaker and composer of (among others) the CDs Father's Love, part 1 and 2

The book *Living in Sonship* helps us to rediscover what God wants to do through us and through His kingdom on earth. It all began with Adam and Eve and the relationship they had with the Father. Thanks to Jesus, it's now possible for us to enter into that (restored) relationship with the Father. We hope this book will also be published in Albanese soon.

Faton Berisha
Victory Church, Gjakova, Kosovo

We have known Henk Bruggeman since 2005. He was one of the first who brought us into contact with the Father love of God. He introduced us to a love that revolutionised our (up until then) spiritual-moralistic living. This love completely transformed our jaded existence into a love relationship with God, based on trust. Henk is not only the bringer of good news, he himself is a joyful expression of the Father heart of God. He joyfully walks the path of his own sonship and at the same time, is one of the most fatherly and dependable people we have come to know within the Father heart movement. We are glad to see that his refreshing and humorous message has finally been made available in book form, hopefully to a large audience.

Martin and Ulla Tenbuß
Employees at 'Team.F', Germany

For many years now, I have been sitting under Henk's inspiring teaching on the Father heart of God. Perhaps I even know his favourite subjects (which are in this book) better than himself! As I am very familiar with the orphan spirit, I regard this baptism of sonship as something more than a revelation: it unleashes a revolution!

Frank Krause
Speaker and writer of (among others) Du sollst leben,
and Haus des Gebets, *Germany*

Contents

Thank you!   9

Foreword   13

Introduction   15

1. How it all began   25

2. The Father Heart of God   35

3. Jesus, the Son of God   43

4. The Parable of the Lost Son   51

5. The Five Wise and the Five Foolish Virgins
and other parables   67

6. The Lost Sheep   83

7. The Orphan   93

8. Peter, James and John   107

9. Do not be afraid   135

10. Two women   147

11. His holy name   161

12. The Father, The Son and Israel   179

Thank you!

It has taken me a very long time to write this book. At different times, I would go out by myself for a few days to work uninterruptedly. Last time, I even went out for eleven straight days, in Egypt, far away from all the bustle of life. My wife, Anneke, has been instrumental in making this possible; she has given herself completely to the care of the family and grandchildren.

I am also very thankful for the ones who have helped me review the manuscript. I would like to thank Hans de Klerk, Henk van Deutekom and Peter Fransen of Great Life Publishing, and Malcolm Down Publishing.

Often people ask me: 'How did you come to the point where you only speak on the revelation of the Father heart of God?' The answer lies in several very significant encounters. I am very thankful for these people and would like to acknowledge them here.

John and Carol Arnott

Since 1994 there has been an outpouring of the Father's love in their church in Toronto. This outpouring has since changed the lives of millions. Anneke and I went to Toronto and were very powerfully touched by God. This was no accident! John and Carol have become examples of true leadership to us, of the way God intended it. This is why we especially want to give thanks to them.

Ian and Janice Ross

In 1994, Ian came from Toronto to the Netherlands, and he still does. Over the years, Ian and I have worked together with great joy. He spoke the very significant prophetic word 'Revivalist, revivalist, revivalist' over me in The Hague in 1998. You can read more on this in the introduction of this book. It set me on the path of becoming an evangelist to the Church, to pass on, through revelation, new things from the Father heart of God. For years, Ian and his wife, Janice, had served side by side with John and Carol in the leadership of the church in Toronto.

Ruth Fazal

Anneke and I have had the privilege of getting to know Ruth personally and have been able to work together several times. Her worship music is known and loved worldwide. Through her many CDs, she has helped thousands of people come into intimacy with the Father. She is also very involved in Israel and is helping the Church find her place there.

Ivan and Isabel Allum

Both Ivan and Isabel have a powerful prophetic ministry. They travel around the whole world, challenging thousands of people and helping them find their destiny. Isabel has spoken multiple times in the Vaderhuis and her prophetic words have deeply impacted many. Their book *Your Destiny* (www.ivan-isabel.com) is an absolute *must-read*!

Partners In Harvest

In 1996, I was at the meeting where *Partners In Harvest* (PIH) was born. It came out of a desire of leaders who had been touched by the outpouring of the love of the Father to meet regularly. I want to thank **Fred and Sharon Wright** and **Dan and Gwen Slade** for their leadership.

Roland and Heidi Baker – Iris Ministries

I know of no missionaries who bear greater fruit from their labour than this couple! They have planted more than 10,000 churches – over 5,000 in Mozambique. They are a great blessing to the Body of Christ worldwide. Anneke and I have travelled several times to Mozambique to visit Iris Ministries. We now travel annually to Matola in Mozambique, where Corrie Ockhuysen runs a home of Iris Ministries, housing around forty children.

Fatherheart Ministries

Around the turn of the last century, **James and Denise Jordan** from New Zealand founded Fatherheart Ministries. They worked together for many years with Jack Winter, one of the pioneers of the revelation of the Father heart of God. James and Denise were also involved with PIH and here Anneke and I first came into contact with their ministry. They are well known through the **Fatherheart Schools** they organise worldwide. Attending one of these schools became a major turning point in our lives.

Finally, I would like to thank **Jeff and Sylvia Scaldwell** from England for their inspiring partnership.

There are, of course, many more people who inspired us, including a great number of writers, but that would make these acknowledgements too long so I will end here. In all the years that we have come to know these people, the following scripture has taken on a very significant meaning for us:

Ephesians 3:17-19:

> *so that Christ may dwell in your hearts through faith.
> And I pray that you, being rooted and established in
> love, may have power,* **together** *with all the Lord's
> holy people, to grasp how wide and long and high and
> deep is the love of Christ, and to know this love that
> surpasses knowledge — that you may be filled to the
> measure of all the fullness of God.*

Be blessed in reading this book.

Henk Bruggeman

Foreword

This is truly a remarkable book. Not just because I have known the author for over thirty-five years, or because I am the publisher of this book, but because it contains extraordinary content. That is why I am especially grateful that we got to publish this book.

This book is not a product of study; it has its origin in day-to-day life, life with God, the Father. Henk writes from his own experiences with God and describes the revelation He has given him. So, this is definitely not a theoretical book, but one written from experience through revelation.

Henk frequently quotes James Jordan by saying: 'Living in sonship with God forms the bookshelf of our life's journey.' The books contain the topics of our life. They rest on the bookshelf of the love of the Father and the sonship He has promised to us. If we don't know this love, we are effectively orphans, even if we have made a choice for God, have been baptised and are active members of the Church. The lost son in Luke 15 was still a son, but he did not live in – and out of – sonship. He was living as an orphan, until he came home to his father. That is the essence of this book: that we can come home to the Father.

I have often heard Henk speak on this topic and every time I discovered something new about God as my Father. For more than thirteen years Henk has spoken on this topic, both on a national and international level. His message has changed many people's lives. That is why I want to invite you to not only read this book, but to really dive in, to submerge yourself in it. Take the chance: it will change your life.

Peter Fransen
Founder of the Ontmoet God foundation and co-owner of Great Life Publishing

Henk Bruggeman has done an incredible job in bringing to us his revelation on what it truly means to live in freedoms as a son as opposed to the opposite, which is living in bondage as a slave. When I was asked to read and consider endorsing this book I have to confess that I wondered why we needed yet another book on the 'Father heart of God' only to discover that this is not just another book on the subject, in fact it is probably the clearest revelation that I have read on this topic.

I myself am an expositor on what it is to walk in intimacy whilst experiencing the love of the Father, and as a result have felt that I had received some deep revelation over the twenty plus years that I have shared on this subject, but to my delight and amazement I have been taken deeper into the heart journey by Henk's own experience and personal walk with 'the Father' and in that respect it is a must-read for everyone wishing to experience the 'Father heart of God' as they did their spiritual conversion – it will change your life forever.

Ken Gott
Senior leader of the House of Prayer Europe

Introduction

I have long considered if I should write a book. So much has already been written, what can be the benefit of yet another book? Nevertheless, I still decided to start writing. All the revelation I have received from the Father heart of God, and the tangible results in the lives of people with whom I shared this revelation, have been the decisive factor to make the step to write this book.

It is wonderful to hear testimonies of people whose lives have been genuinely transformed. What comes to mind is first my own life and the life of my wife, Anneke. But also, the lives of Maria, John, Theo and Petra and many, many others. For some, their entire faith was turned upside down, and others even got angry and said: 'Why wasn't I told this sooner . . .?'

This book is not written for study. It is also not meant to be a manual for a 'new method'. It is to give guidance, in the same way that a road sign helps you find the right way to a certain city. The most important thing is to reach your destination and to enjoy the journey to it. The road signs are not the destination, they are merely a helpful tool. And that is my intention with this book: that it would be a helpful tool.

Anneke has always helped me to stay balanced on this journey: 'It is great what you're saying, but how does it practically work, at home?' Practicality doesn't always make it easy for me, but it does make sure that whatever I teach is real. Together we climb mountains, and go through valleys. One thing we both know: it is the Father who helps us through it all, and together we desire to move forward.

Larissa's testimony

Larissa was a young German woman. I met her and her husband for the first time at a Father heart conference in Germany. Later she told me that initially, she did not want to come to this conference. Her husband literally dragged her to it. In fact, Larissa had lost the desire to live.

Larissa testified: 'The first nine years of my life we lived in Kyrgyzstan. We then moved to Germany, where we settled into new our lives. I grew up as the third child, having seven brothers and sisters. My parents didn't want to have that many children because with every pregnancy, our cares only increased. Throughout my entire childhood, I always had the feeling of being rejected. Rejected by my parents, because they didn't have time for me, but also by my brothers and sisters, because for the one I was too young and for the other I was too old. I was often alone.

I tried in my own strength to live a holy life, but time after time I failed miserably.

'From a young age, we were told to give our lives to the Lord, otherwise we would end up in hell. That is why, as a teenager – motivated by the fear of going to hell – I gave my life to the Lord many times at evangelical crusades. I tried in my own strength to live a holy life, but time after time I failed miserably. Every time I sinned I thought that God stopped loving me, because He hates sin. In my attempts to please God and failing every time, my feelings of rejection became increasingly stronger and I became a depressed teenager.

'When I was fifteen years old, my dad had an encounter with God. That transformed him completely. Suddenly he was able to tell us he loved us, and much more than that.

Everyone in our family experienced this change, including myself! And that is what I wanted too! I wanted to have a genuine encounter with God, through which I would really know that I was His child.

'At the age of eighteen I decided to get baptised, in the hope that through this, I would get closer to God. This, however, did not happen. I finished school and spent a year at Bible school. Here I met many other Christians. They were so free, totally different from what I had known up until then. I only knew the "works of righteousness" (see Titus 3:5, AMP): to do good and not to sin. But I also wanted to be free. I wanted a life of joy, not of fear.

'In October 1997, I once again surrendered my life to the Lord. I had a strong expectation that He would completely transform my life. And this time it happened, I had a wondrous encounter with my Lord. All my burdens left me and I felt light as a feather, and: accepted! I had finally found my Lord. I could barely wait to go home and tell my parents that I had made a new decision for the Lord. In the past I would have felt embarrassed and wouldn't want to tell anyone, but at that moment I would have gladly told the whole world.

'Eleven years went by with ups and downs. A new-found trust in God was growing, the One for whom nothing was impossible. My father placed us under the protection of God every single day, ensuring that no great harm should befall us. Unfortunately, something did happen. In September 2008, my brother had a motorbike accident. He had a head-on collision with a bus. He went straight up to his heavenly Father. He went home and did not look back.

'I decided to rededicate myself to the church I attended at that time, and thought about how I could be doing more for the kingdom of God. *One year and three months later* one of my good friends took his own life. For a second time my life completely collapsed. Depression and sorrow over the loss of my brother and my friend ruled my life. I did not want to live any longer, but I was too afraid to end it myself. Wonderful events, like getting to know and marry my husband, did not help me to make a turn-around. My life was still full of sorrow and depression.

'In October 2012, my husband literally dragged me to a Father heart conference with Henk. Moved by the Father's love Henk spoke about and emanated, I wept incessantly. He told me about other Father heart conferences that were held on a ship called the *Siloam*. I knew I needed to go; that is where my life would change.

> **I arrived on the Siloam depressed and turned inward, and a few days later went home filled with joy and hope!**

'In the summer of 2013, the long-expected change happened. I arrived on the Siloam depressed and turned inward, and a few days later went home filled with joy and hope! I cannot exactly pinpoint what happened there, but an encounter with the Father changed everything. He took the sorrow and depression out of my life and returned to me my joy. Suddenly it was good that my brother was with Him and not here on earth.

'This experience got me thinking about the meaning of life. What did I live for? What was God's purpose for my life? What was my destiny? At the next boat conference with Henk, the Father answered me: "To be my daughter, that is the meaning of your life!" What a joy! The Father wanted me as His daughter. I am no longer an orphan and I am no longer rejected. I am His daughter! I do not have to strive for it, I can simply be His daughter. He healed all my wounds and now teaches me how to be His daughter. That is what the Father is like! He is so amazing and knows us all so well. He knows our desires.

'My first-born son, Ruben, was a huge gift. He came into the world seven years after the death of my brother, as the seventh grandson of my parents, born the exact same day when I saw my brother for the last time. My son is not a replacement for my brother, but he is a huge gift from a heavenly Father to his daughter. Words cannot express what this means to me, to receive such a wonderful gift. How loving, then, is such a Father, who planned everything and saw all the days that were so important to me. I am certain that He also was very excited for the moment that I would discover His surprise for me.'

The mind does not having feelings: the heart does!

As I mentioned before, the purpose of this book is to give guidance. Only reading it is not enough. It is not my intention that we should learn more about God in our minds, but that we would experience Him more in our lives, in our hearts. And this will be, for everyone, a personal experience. This way we really get to know the God who calls Himself our Father.

This is a book in which you will occasionally make a surprising discovery, teaching you new things about the Father. Or you might find that He is very different from what you have always thought Him to be. It is my desire that these discoveries will bring you to a place of deeper, more personal intimacy with the Father.

This book is not just about revelation, in the sense of receiving *new* insights, it is also about revealing *wrong* insights. This can be very liberating. We want to see the

> **This is a book in which you will occasionally make a surprising discovery ...**

Church, or rather ourselves, from a new perspective. Thus, we will approach from two different angles. On the one hand, we will discover who God the Father truly is. On the other: *the yet to be discovered (or not yet revealed) potential in us.*

It is important in this process to let go of your own trusted insights and to be prepared to trust Him in absolutely everything. From independence to total dependence. That is the path in front of us. When this becomes a reality to us, 'the Church' will also be completely transformed!

Revivalist

I think it was 1998 when Ian Ross (a speaker from Canada) visited our church in The Hague for a few days. In this time, I was wrestling with some unanswered questions. I had been a Christian for more than twenty years and was from the start very active in my faith. In our time with the Jesus People, the emphasis was on evangelisation. Later, when we got involved with Youth With a Mission, teaching and missions were the central theme. I was aware of the five-fold ministry, but still I asked myself the question: 'What am I, exactly?'

I was not a real evangelist, my heart was not for the streets, so to speak. A teacher, then? I had studied teaching, but to become a full-time teacher seemed quite uninteresting to me; it was not adventurous enough. A prophet, then? I wanted to become more prophetic but I didn't see myself as a prophet! A shepherd? Never! I didn't want to become a church leader and be tied down to a congregation, constantly having pastoral conversations with needy people. An apostle, then?

My view of an apostle was someone who travelled around and planted new churches everywhere. This too did not fit me.

But then Ian came! After one of the meetings there was a time of receiving personal prayer. A moment came that he stood next to me and spoke these prophetic words over me: 'Revivalist, revivalist, revivalist.' From that moment

I asked myself: What am I, exactly?

on, I knew. I longed to be involved with 'revival'. I loved to be an 'evangelist for the Church'. To challenge people. To challenge Christians who had lost hope, to start believing again. To question 'set' ways and look together for the renewal of the Church.

I was also becoming increasingly aware that this renewal of the Church could not be brought forth out of self-effort or by new ideas. I discovered that the basis for renewal lies in the revelation we receive from the Father heart of God. Only through the revelation of the Father heart is it possible for us to come into true sonship.

Ecclesia

When we talk in this book about 'the congregation' or 'the Church', I predominantly mean the Body of Christ, not the Church as an institution. It is important to note here that the word *ecclesia,* which in the New Testament is translated to *church or assembly,* means *a small group or community of believers.*

Throughout this book, we will encounter new ways of thinking about the Church, and there may be occasions where I'll shine a new light on who God the Father really is. I hope that by reading this book you will be encouraged.

My desire is to impart the revelation that has been given to me. Throughout the book a picture is painted of God's plan with the Church, with us and with you! But this is merely a picture. It is truly my desire that by the reading of this book you will come into new intimacy with the Father. That you will receive a new revelation of the Father heart of God.

At the end of each chapter, and in other places, I have written 'time to reflect'. When you read this, if you can, put down the book for a while. Do not just keep on reading, take a moment to reflect on what you have just read and try to see its relevance in your own life.

> **Meeting the Father doesn't happen in your head and mind, but in your heart.**

At the end of each chapter I will often suggest a CD of a certain musician. We have found that through music, you can get in touch with your heart. Meeting the Father doesn't happen in your head and mind, but in your heart. He will often speak to your heart. After having read a chapter, it is good to take time to reflect on what you have just read. It is important to allow the words to drop down from your mind into your heart. We will see that when God touches our heart, filling us with love, our thinking is also transformed.

And so, I have written this book for anyone. Anyone who hungers and thirsts for more.

Time to reflect:

What a beautiful testimony from Larissa and what a privilege it is to know that God wants to be a Father to you in a unique way. The challenge lies before us; you also can start on your adventure.

To listen:

Chuck Girard, 'Enter In'

Additional reading:

Wayne Jacobsen, *Finding Church* (Amsterdam, Netherlands: Blue Sheep Media, 2014)

Space for notes/reflections:

ONE

How it all began

Genesis 1:26-27 (*The Message*):

God spoke:

*'Let us make human beings in our image,
make them reflecting our nature . . .'*

*God created human beings; he created them godlike,
Reflecting God's nature.
He created them male and female.*

Creation

If we want to discover God's plan for humanity, we must look at creation. Here we immediately see that God created human beings very different from the other creatures. The creation of animals looks somewhat of a common or impersonal nature. The creation of man, however, has very personal and distinct characteristics. Moreover, there is something very important that distinguishes man from everything else in creation: the ability to live in *intimacy* with God.

God created man with the intention of them being the crown of His creation. Not simply as a created being separate from Himself, but in true intimacy: He wants to be one with man. He wants to share His life with man, and He desires to enjoy the Fatherhood He has for His children to the fullest.

Genesis 2:7:

> Then the Lord God formed a man from the dust of the
> ground and breathed into his nostrils the breath of
> life, and the man became a living being.

The image of God

Where was Eve when God created humankind? He created
Adam, the human, containing both male *and* female. Eve
was, as it were, still hidden in Adam. For this reason, it is
important to see that *together* they formed the image of
God. The man and the woman together form the image
of God.

Genesis 1:27-28:

> So God created mankind in his own image, in the image
> of God he created them; male and female he created
> them. God blessed them and said to them, 'Be fruitful
> and increase in number; fill the earth and subdue it.
> Rule over the fish in the sea and the birds in the sky and
> over every living creature that moves on the ground.'

Genesis 2:15-18:

> The Lord God took the man and put him in the Garden
> of Eden to work it and take care of it. And the Lord God
> commanded the man, 'You are free to eat from any tree
> in the garden; but you must not eat from the tree of the
> knowledge of good and evil, for when you eat from it you
> will certainly die.' The Lord God said, 'It is not good for the
> man to be alone. I will make a helper suitable for him.'

It is wonderful that here we first see a perfect unity
displaying the image of God. Mankind, male *and* female in

complete unity. Created in the image of God the Father, the Son and the Holy Spirit, all three forming a perfect union. We then see that He takes the woman, as it were, out of the man, and says: 'Look, mankind first existing in complete oneness, has now become two individuals, man and woman'. And the beautiful thing is that now, through love, they can become one again, after the image of their Maker.

By the way, did you know that the Hebrew language has characters that at the same time also represent numbers? When you add up the numeric value of the text 'the Lord our God, the Lord is one' (Deuteronomy 6:4), you get the number 111. This is a beautiful depiction of the Trinity.

Be fruitful and increase in number

Have you ever considered why God only created Adam and Eve this way? Why didn't He create all human beings in the same manner? He could create ten every week, or even 100. But no, He gave mankind the ability to procreate. Why? I think His reason was that He didn't want to keep us from the wonderful experience of parenthood. What an incredible moment it is, when you bring a son or daughter into the world and you realise that part of yourself is now being represented in a new creation, one that you can cherish and brings you love! This is the same experience the Father had when he created Adam and Eve, His children. He wants to share this with us.

The Fall

Genesis 2:21-23:

So the Lord God caused the man to fall into a deep sleep; and while he was sleeping, he took one of the man's ribs and then closed up the place with flesh. Then the Lord God made a woman from the rib he had taken out of the man, and he brought her to the man. The man said, 'This is now bone of my bones and flesh of my flesh; she shall be called "woman", for she was taken out of man.'

Now Eve is walking through the garden and suddenly she hears a voice speaking to her (Genesis 3:1-7). Looking up she sees a snake in the trees. This snake says to her: 'God probably told you that you're not allowed to eat from the fruit of the trees, didn't He?' 'No', says Eve. 'He didn't say that at all. We can eat of every fruit of the trees. However, what a coincidence, there is one exception, and that's the tree you're in; the tree of the knowledge of good and evil.'

> **God probably told you that you're not allowed to eat from the fruit of the trees, didn't He?**

'Well, I know why you're not allowed to eat from this tree because it will make you like God!' answers the snake. At this point, Eve could have easily said: 'Now, listen here, we are in Genesis 3, but if you come back with me to Genesis 1, you will see clearly that God created mankind in His image and likeness. I don't have to do anything to become like God, I already am!'

How can it be that the snake was able to tempt Eve with these words? What does this temptation consist of? It is utterly important that you understand this, because the snake tried the very same thing on Jesus and he is still trying to tempt us today in this same way. His only goal is to disrupt the unity between God the Father and His creation; His children. Of course, Satan knows that God created man 'in his own image', but what he in essence is saying to Eve is this: 'You can become like God without being dependent on Him!'

Independence is the root of all sin. It has become deeply ingrained in our entire existence. Many people find it difficult to desire dependency. This is understandable. All of us have had bad experiences when it comes to trusting and being dependent on other people. That's why it is important to understand that there is an unhealthy and a healthy type of dependence. With unhealthy dependence, the other person is trying to benefit from the relationship at your cost. Control and manipulation often play a part in this. With healthy dependence, your safety, development and well-being are central. In your dependence upon God the Father, He makes it possible for you to enter the fullness of your destiny.

God the Father creates Adam and Eve out of an intense desire to share His love.

Sonship

We now see the following happen to Adam and Eve: living in a secure environment, safe in the presence and intimacy of God the Father, they make the decision to walk away from this place. Let's pause for a moment and take a look at what's really happening here. God the *Father* creates Adam and Eve out of an intense desire to share His love. His intention is that it doesn't stop with these two children, but that they will multiply. God's plan is that He will be a Father to all. He will care for them. In unity with Him, they will come into the fullness of their destiny which is kept for them.

Adam is not merely a creature of God, he receives sonship! I believe this is one of the most important truths we are receiving revelation on today. Our salvation has been the central theme for a long time. We give our lives to Jesus; our sins are forgiven and we move from the kingdom of darkness into the kingdom of light. You become a child of God. Next, we try to grow as Christians through good biblical teaching and by being involved with a church or community.

But when God created Adam, He didn't start with teaching or work. He started with intimacy, with building a relationship. God breathed the breath of life into Adam's nostrils and he opened his eyes for the first time. Can you imagine? This is no routine job for God the Father, He has reached the final crescendo, 'The Grand Finale', the crown of His creation . . . mankind! From the dust He has formed him, and there he lies, motionless, until He breathes the breath of life into Adam's nostrils. Then God holds His breath and waits until Adam opens his eyes. Everything in God rejoices; He is delighted, proud, happy. His heart almost bursts of love and compassion.

And Adam? From the moment he opens his eyes, he looks straight into the eyes of the Father. In these eyes, he sees the love of a Father who loves him with everything that is in Him. And he drinks it in; he is not only a child of God, here he receives sonship, completely!

The sixth day

Have you ever considered the order in which God created the world? I once heard a man – Paul Nedoszytko from Bath – speak on this. It was only at the end of creation, the sixth day, that God created man. Why not the first day, so that man would have been involved with everything that God does? But no, God decides to create man on the sixth day and after this comes the seventh day, the day of rest.

Does God need this day because He is tired and exhausted? I can't imagine that. Did He do it, then, for man? Man hadn't done anything yet, for him it is only the first day after his creation. Man starts off with a day of rest!

This way God ensures that man doesn't associate Him primarily with work. On the day of rest, the Father focuses on relationship and intimacy with His children.

Man starts off with a day of rest!

Conversion and then, moving forward ...

You can draw a comparison between the moment we are converted and the moment Adam was created. He is a child of God from the moment he is created, but he only receives the identity of sonship through experiencing the intimacy and love of the Father, by drinking it in.

When we come to Jesus and kneel at His feet, we receive the forgiveness of sins through the finished work of the cross. We become a new creation. We are then born again of the Spirit. Many Christians believe that with this experience they have reached their final destination. This is not true. What in fact has happened, is that now we have been given *the ability* to reach our destination!

John 10:9:

> *I am the gate; whoever enters through me will be saved. They will come in and go out, and find pasture.*

It's important to know that when you get born again, it happens more or less automatically. Just like a natural birth, which doesn't come about by any effort of the baby. In like manner, we also receive new life by being born again.

But this is not our destination. Jesus says: 'I am the gate.' We can adore the gate, and tell others how wonderful the gate is. We can even promise to never leave the gate. But a gate is something you travel through, it gives you access to something you otherwise would never be able to reach! And Jesus continues.

John 14:6:

> Jesus answered, 'I am the way and the truth and the life. **No one comes to the Father except through me.'**

This tells us that there are different stages. First, we hear the gospel. It tells us of the Father, the Son and the Holy Spirit.

Romans 10:14:

> How, then, can they call on the one they have not believed in? And how can they believe in the one of whom they have not heard? And how can they hear without someone preaching to them?

Then comes believing . . .

Ephesians 2:8:

> For it is by grace you have been saved, through faith – and this is not from yourselves, **it is the gift of God** . . .

This is how we find Jesus who gives us new life. But he gives it with a purpose.

John 3:5-6:

> Jesus answered, 'Very truly I tell you, no one can enter the kingdom of God unless they are born of water and

*the Spirit. Flesh gives birth to flesh, **but the Spirit gives birth to spirit.***

Because we are now born of the Spirit, it is once again possible for us to come into relationship with God the Father, He who is also Spirit.

John 4:24:

> ***God is spirit**, and his worshippers must worship in the Spirit and in truth.*

Now we have arrived at our true destination: the arms of the Father, who welcomes us gladly. Welcome home!

Matthew 10:39:

> *Whoever finds their life will lose it, and whoever loses their life for my sake will find it.*

Time to reflect:

Let's take some time to reflect on our faith journey and see if we recognise the moment we came home to the Father. Are you still at the gate? Why don't you step on through? Jesus also says He is 'the way' (John 14:6). He loves to journey with you and to introduce you to His Father.

To listen:

John Nuttall, 'Welcome Home'

Additional reading:

Barry Adams, 'Father's Love Letter', http://www.fatherslove letter.com/

Jack Winter, *The Homecoming* (Edmonds, WA: YWAM Publishing, 1999)

Space for notes/reflections:

T W O

The Father Heart of God

Jeremiah 31:3 (*The Message*):

*God told them: 'I've never quit loving you and
never will. Expect love, love and more love!'*

The garden

Ever since the year 2002, whenever I'm invited to speak at
meetings, I only speak on the revelation of the Father heart
of God. That is quite some time. The core of this message
has not changed since then, but new revelation is continually
being added. It's continually enlarging and keeps going deeper.

To expound on this, I will draw a comparison between this
revelation and a garden. If you live in a city, you will really
enjoy having a little garden at the back of your house. Every
season has its own charms and if you look for it, you will
always discover something new. You will really enjoy the
warm summer sun, the glorious colours of the autumn
leaves, the serene beauty of an unspoiled bed of snow in the
winter, and the arrival of new life in the spring. Magnificent!

When you own a mansion with a plot of forest, you will
have a different experience in your 'garden'. You can go for
long walks and there will be much more to discover. With
the sunlight breaking through the canopy, it is delightful to
sit down in a bed of moss under the shade of a giant oak.

Now, what if your garden was the size of an entire country? You would be able to wander around and take a different route every day of the year. One day you would go to the beach to see the ocean, the next day you would float down a river in the mountains. You would enjoy the fruit from the orchards, only to go for a nice swim in the lake at the end of the day.

This how I envision the Father heart of God. Many people say: 'The Father heart of God? I know about that one.' What they often mean is, they have enjoyed the little garden at the back of their house. There is more, so much more.

New revelation

When I'm invited to speak somewhere, people often say: 'How is it possible that we missed this, that we didn't see it before?' I have discovered that we cannot learn this truth by study or our own effort. We are dependent on revelation, a revelation directly from the Father heart of God. When we impart this revelation to others, it is like a veil being lifted, enabling them to see and discover new things.

We are dependent on revelation . . .

In the Bible, there are often mysteries mentioned that are unveiled or made known by revelation.

Ephesians 3:2-4:

*Surely you have heard about the administration of God's grace that was given to me for you, that is, **the mystery made known to me by revelation,** as I have already written briefly. In reading this, then, you will be able to understand my insight into the mystery of Christ . . .*

In other places, there is mention of doors being opened and keys being given.

I believe that in this (end)time, the Father wants to reveal many mysteries again. Teaching and preaching will in the times ahead be energised by revelation. God is at this moment looking for people to whom He can give keys to open doors, and so enter new territory.

Over the years something else has come to my attention: whenever a new revelation comes into the Christian world, it will often be presented as something you can join. A new movement, where you leave the 'old' and embrace the 'new'. With the revelation of the Father heart of God I find that the exact opposite is true.

I visit many different denominations. From Anglican to Pentecostal, from Protestant Reformed to Evangelical. Every Christian has a certain view of God and knows that he is a Father. For the one, it might already be a substantial garden, for the other, this view is still limited to a flowerpot, with or without blossoming flowers. But I always find a starting point. Then I am able to continue and talk about the new revelation that *joins onto this one.* I don't have tell them: 'Listen, you have to join a new movement if you want to advance in the Father heart of God.' On the contrary, the Father wants to meet you in the place you are right now, making Himself known to you. And that is unique.

Revelation through experience

I believe we now have a key to discover the love of the Father. We must realise that we need a revelation and that we receive this revelation through experience.

In the parable of the lost son in Luke 15, the prodigal son makes the decision to return to his father. But there is more needed than just making the right choice. The son will not experience being restored in sonship by his decision. He says: 'I am not worthy of being called your son' (see verse 19).Only when he feels the embrace of his father's arms will the love of his father be revealed to him. Knowledge or effort were not able to reveal it to him. Paul writes about this in his letter to the Ephesians.

Ephesians 3:17-19:

> so that Christ may dwell in your hearts through faith. And I pray that you, being rooted and established in love, may have power, together with all the Lord's holy people, to grasp how wide and long and high and deep is the **love of Christ**, and to know this love that surpasses knowledge – that you may be filled to the measure of all the fullness of God.

The Amplified Bible states the following:

> and [that you may come] to know [**practically, through personal experience**] the love of Christ which far surpasses [**mere**] **knowledge without experience** . . .

The love of God the Father exceeds all understanding, it is simply unfathomable. But what the mind cannot fathom, the heart can. Just like you are unable to express in words 'being in love', but you are able to enjoy to the fullest this intense happiness deep in your heart. It is the same with the love of the Father: you can experience and enjoy Him!

The love of God the Father exceeds all understanding . . .

The photo and the Bible

When my mother was born in Amsterdam in 1923, her father was not home. He worked in the navy and was stationed for some years in Indonesia, at that time a Dutch colony. In their house, on the mantelpiece, there was a photo of her father. Every evening her mother said to her: 'Riek, it is time for bed, give Daddy a kiss.' She would walk over to the photo, kiss the photo and was then put to bed.

Then the time came that her father returned home. He would sit in the living room and it would be my mother's bedtime. Her mother said, 'Give Daddy a kiss', and she would walk straight passed him to the mantelpiece and kiss the photo.

In some ways the Bible is similar to a photo. In a photo, you see the colour of their hair, the shape of their nose, the eyes, the ears and the mouth. With a photo, you get an idea of what the actual person looks like. In the same way the is Bible a picture of God. But looking at a picture or reading about someone is very different from actually meeting the person. Could it be that while we read the Bible, the Father is present in the same room, longing for a personal connection with us?

No carved image

In the Ten Commandments, it says that we are not allowed to make a carved image of God. One day I suddenly understood that we shouldn't be reading this with the emphasis on the prohibition, but that we must look at this from the perspective of God's heart. What He says here is: 'I do not want you to get a wrong impression of who I am! I am your Father and I don't want you to miss this reality by replacing Me with a carved image.'

Genesis 1:26:

> *Then God said, 'Let us make mankind in our image, in our likeness, so that they may rule over the fish in the sea and the birds in the sky, over the livestock and all the wild animals, and over all the creatures that move along the ground.'*

We see here that God has laid His image in us. We have been made to be God's image. Every other image, from which the life of God has been taken away, gives us a completely wrong impression of who God really is.

This is one of those scriptures that can give you a wrong idea about who God is. You can read the Ten Commandments and get the impression that He is a God who tells you what you can and cannot do. He is in charge and you must learn to listen and obey. I now read this passage from the perspective of a loving Father, who wants to make sure His children don't get a wrong impression of Him, because He is longing to be known for who He really is!

The Father heart of God and sonship

God's deepest desire is to be Father.

God's deepest desire is to be Father. But to be able to really be a Father, you need to have children you can care for: sons and daughters. From the beginning this has been His desire . . .

Jeremiah 3:19:

> *I thought you would call me 'Father'*
> *and not turn away from following me.*

Time to reflect:

Take some time to open your heart. The Father welcomes you with open arms. He says: 'You are my son, my daughter, and I love you.' How much have you received from the Father heart of God? How big is your 'garden'? There is *always* more!

To listen:

John Nuttall, 'Try Running'

Additional reading:

James Jordan, *Sonship: A Journey Into Father's Heart* (Wellington, NZ: The National Library of New Zealand, 2nd edition 2014)

Space for notes/reflections:

THREE

Jesus, the Son of God

John 1:14 (*The Message*):

The Word became flesh and blood, and moved into the neighborhood. We saw the glory with our own eyes, the one-of-a-kind glory, like Father, like Son, Generous inside and out, true from start to finish.

Jesus came to earth

After the downfall of Adam and Eve, with all its unfortunate consequences, we have now arrived at the time of Jesus, the Son of God. His coming is a turning point in history. He came to restore what was lost. He came to show us what it is like to live in total dependency on the Father and in close unity with Him.

It is imperative that we see matters clearly. When we look at what Jesus did, we can surely say that He lived without sin. You can also say that because of this, He became the perfect sacrifice and that through His blood, through His death on the cross, salvation and forgiveness of sins have been made available for us. This is evidently true, but there is a much deeper reality.

Basically, Jesus came to restore – for the entire human race – the wrong choices Adam and Eve had made. This was His highest purpose in coming to earth as a man. By erasing sin, it has now become possible for us to inhabit the place

God originally intended for us. For this reason, Jesus makes a very clear statement in John 5. He says: 'I can do nothing by Myself, I am completely dependent on the Father.'

John 5:19:

> Jesus gave them this answer: 'Very truly I tell you, the Son can do nothing by himself; he can do only what he sees his Father doing, because whatever the Father does the Son also does.'

Later, in John 20, Jesus says He lived His life as an example for us and challenges us to live the same life.

John 20:21:

> Again Jesus said, 'Peace be with you! As the Father has sent me, I am sending you.'

Jesus, the Son of God, came to earth as a man. This is something (almost) all of us reading know. But it is important to look beyond mere intellectual understanding. I recently started to understand in a deep way the extraordinary nature of what happened here.

No one knows the Father ...

The affair of every religion is man trying to get closer to God. This, however, demands effort and you will often be urged to try your very best. How different is it in our relationship with God as Father? *He* takes the initiative to come up with a rescue plan, so that His children will get to know Him again. This restores the relationship so that He can be a Father of many children.

All that went wrong in the beginning, Jesus will restore again. 'In the beginning' (Genesis 1:1) God created man with spirit, soul and body. Through the Fall we have been alienated from God. This caused our spirit, as it were, to fall into a coma. We lack in spirit. But it is through the spirit, not through the flesh, that we can come into relationship with God.

John 4:24:

> God is spirit, and his worshippers must worship in the Spirit and in truth.

1 Corinthians 2:14:

> The person without the Spirit does not accept the things that come from the Spirit of God but considers them foolishness, and cannot understand them because they are discerned only through the Spirit.

God knows that no matter how much He longs for His children, their lacking in spirit is an insuperable problem for Him to come into relationship with them. For this same reason, it is virtually impossible for us to know what He is really like. We need revelation from Jesus!

Matthew 11:27:

> All things have been committed to me by my Father. No one knows the Son except the Father, **and no one knows the Father except the Son and those to whom the Son chooses to reveal him**.

This is quite a statement Jesus makes here. It is a powerful statement! Here it says that we cannot know the Father by ourselves. It is for this very reason that the Father asked Jesus to (temporarily) lay aside the benefits of His divinity and become man. This has never happened in any other religion. Instead of asking us to climb higher, Jesus comes down to become one of us.

We have just read in John 4 that God is spirit. It is pretty obvious that the Holy Spirit is also spirit. But Jesus too, was like this, before He became man. The Father asked Jesus, who is spirit, to become flesh and become equal to men. God becomes a man. It is almost unbelievable!

> **God becomes a man. It is almost unbelievable!**

Why is this so important?

After mankind had been separated from God by sin, it was now impossible for man-in-the-flesh to have relationship with God, who is spirit. Now Jesus comes to live among us in the flesh, as a man. And because He was always without sin, it was possible for Him to be one with the Father, as a man. Because He only did what He saw the Father doing, and only spoke the words He heard the Father speak, it was possible for the people around Him, through Him, to see the Father. And so, it has become possible for us, as well, to really get to know the Father for the first time.

Ephesians 1:17-18:

> *I keep asking that the God of our Lord Jesus Christ, the glorious Father, may give you the **Spirit of wisdom and revelation, so that you may know him better**. I pray that the eyes of your heart may be enlightened **in order that you may know the hope to which he has called you**, the riches of his glorious inheritance in his holy people . . .*

The best way to get to know God is to have a personal encounter with Him. When we are connected to God's Spirit, our spirit comes alive again. This is also beautifully reflected at the end of the parable of the lost son. Here it is the father saying to his oldest son:

Luke 15:32:

But we had to celebrate and be glad, because this brother of yours was dead and is alive again; he was lost and is found.

Through intimacy with God we receive our identity, making it possible to reach our destiny. Jesus was not only the Son of God, He also continuously walked in sonship. After the Fall, Adam was only able to pass on life to his descendants in the flesh. But now with Jesus, He can restore us again by giving us a new, living spirit.

Through intimacy with God we receive our identity . . .

In the first letter to the Corinthians it says that He is the last Adam. He has come to open the way back to the Father. It was not God's intention that through Christ we would come into a new religion, but into a new relationship. This is the plan of a Father who passionately longs to be united with His children.

1 Corinthians 15:45:

So it is written: 'The first man Adam became a living being'; the last Adam, a life-giving spirit.

The veil is torn

When Jesus died on the cross, something extraordinary happened in the temple. The veil covering the Holy of Holies tore from top to bottom.

In 1 Kings 6:2 it says that Solomon's temple was thirty cubits high. But Josephus Flavius, a historian from the first century AD tells us that King Herod increased the height to forty cubits (this is around twenty metres!) Josephus also mentions that this veil was four inches thick and that even if you tied horses to both ends of the veil, they would not be able to tear it apart![1]

It had to be clear that God wanted to declare something. But for the people who lived in those days, it was very hard to accept. This was a matter of the temple, the place where the Most High lives. He had written all the temple regulations Himself, they were not to be changed! The temple was still in operation until it was destroyed by the Romans in AD70. It is very plausible that the priests would have restored the veil again after it had been torn.

The explanation often given of the veil being torn is that now we can enter in, to come into the presence of God. I believe that the veil being torn much more strongly indicates that God could come out, to meet us. He no longer wants to live in a house of stone, built by human hands. He chooses to have His home in the hearts of His children.

This is a Father, who with a great longing in His eyes, desires to be united with His children, whom He misses so much. All this time He has longed to hold us in His arms and whisper in our ears: 'I love you, you are my beloved son, you are my beloved daughter!'

From the moment the veil was torn in the temple, God changed His course of action. Or better yet, everything that

---

1. Ryrie Study Bible. Note Ex. 26:31-35 (Chicago, IL: Moody Publishers).

happened before had been working towards this moment. Jesus did not come to turn the Jewish religion into a Christian religion. The torn veil is telling us: 'The time of the temple is over; the time of religion is finished!' Instead, it is now possible for us to come into relationship with Father God, and, God is now able to show His children who He can be for them; a Father. Relationship instead of religion.

Psalm 18:20-24 (*The Message*):

> *God made my life complete when I placed all the pieces before him. When I got my act together, he gave me a fresh start. Now I'm alert to God's ways; I don't take God for granted. Every day I review the ways he works; I try not to miss a trick. I feel put back together, and I'm watching my step.* **God rewrote the text of my life when I opened the book of my heart to his eyes.**

Time to reflect:

The Father longs for you, and . . . you can come as you are. The changes will happen later. A new start? It can happen today!

To listen:

Paul Baloche, 'Loved By You'

Additional reading:

Darin Hufford, *The Misunderstood God* (London: Hodder Windblown, 2009)

Space for notes/reflections:

FOUR

The Parable of the Lost Son

Luke 15:20-22 (*The Message*):

When he was still a long way off, his father saw him. His heart pounding, he ran out, embraced him, and kissed him. The son started his speech: 'Father, I've sinned against God, I've sinned before you; I don't deserve to be called your son ever again.' But the father wasn't listening.

Parables

After having seen how Adam and Eve fell and that through Jesus, restoration has been made available, we will now take a look at our own position. In the New Testament, we see that Jesus often speaks in parables. These narratives are meant to be examples to teach us something. That's why it is important to not only read these parables as a nice story, but that we understand the meaning behind the story.

Lost and being found again

In Luke 15 we find the parable of the lost son as the last in a series of three parables. The first parable is that of the lost sheep and the second one is about a lost coin. Firstly, it is good to realise that the headings at the top of each parable were not there in the original text. These titles have been added in later by Bible translators and to some degree reflect the way they looked at these parables. The titles emphasise 'being lost', but the good news is that in every one of these parables, that which was lost has been found again!

For me personally, I don't believe there is any other story in the Bible that has more revelation on the love of the Father and the Father heart of God, than the parable of the lost son.

Ever since that moment in 2002 when I've only been speaking on the revelation of the Father heart of God, I can't remember any time that I haven't cited this parable in one way or another. And the amazing thing is that new revelation keeps coming, it almost seems an inexhaustible well.

Alright, let us have a look at this parable. First it is important to know who the people in the parable are representative of. Let's start with the father. It is pretty obvious that we are talking about God the Father. The next one is the youngest son, who is called 'the lost son'. Who is Jesus signifying here? Can *we* identify ourselves in one way or another with him?

We become a child of God the moment we give our lives to Jesus. That is the moment of conversion. In the conferences and seminars I run, I will often pose the question of what the exact moment was of conversion in this parable. The first response I usually get is the moment the youngest son becomes remorseful when he is with the pigs. Others choose the moment he starts heading home. And others again find the moment the father embraces the son the most comparable to conversion. The moment of receiving the mantle is also sometimes mentioned.

The question is, do these events in the parable really represent the conversion which for us is that moment of being born again? What does the young man ask his father just before he leaves? Exactly, he asks for his share in the inheritance.

Luke 15:12:

> *The younger one said to his father, 'Father, give me my share of the estate.' So he divided his property between them.*

What the son does here is not right. It shows that the son has absolutely no respect for his father, but at the same time, it confirms his identity of a son. The request of the son, and the response of the father, both show that the son doesn't have to become something more, further on in the parable. This means that the parable is meant for Christians and not so much for those in the world who haven't yet given their lives to the Lord. It is telling us that we can be a child of God and still be living separated from Father God.

How do you experience relationship with the Father?

How do you experience relationship with the Father?

(Time to reflect)

Adam and Eve

In this parable, we can also see a resemblance with the story of Adam and Eve. As they chose to become like God *without being dependent* on Him, likewise, the youngest son asks for his share of the inheritance so that he can do what he likes *without being dependent* on his father.

Very often we think that the moment of conversion means that we 'have arrived', and that we don't have to advance any further. Sure, we can grow a bit more as Christians, but a real change is not necessary anymore, is it? That indeed

53

is the question. Jesus tells us that He is the only way to the Father.

John 14:6:

> *Jesus answered, 'I am the way and the truth and the life. No one comes to the Father except through me.'*

Coming to Jesus or, if you like, becoming a Christian, makes it possible for us to start the journey towards our true destination: to be restored in our relationship with the Father!

Someone once asked me: 'Is it necessary to also accept the Father?' This question got me thinking. We commonly believe that we are supposed to accept Jesus at our conversion. Do we then only receive Jesus, or also the Holy Spirit and the Father?

(Time to reflect)

The Trinity is inseparable; therefore, we do not just receive one part, but the whole of the Trinity. But, after our conversion we still we talk about being filled with the Holy Spirit. That's strange, isn't it? I thought we already received Him.

I would like to explain this as follows: at our conversion we meet Jesus personally, though the Holy Spirit and the Father are also present. When we get filled with the Holy Spirit, we are now personally being introduced to Him. If that is the case, then the Father is also waiting for a specific moment at which He can personally introduce Himself to us. And the way He loves to do this is to wrap His arms around us, holding us tightly, filling us with His love and whispering in our ear: 'Do you know how much I love you? You are my beloved son, you are my beloved daughter!'

Returning to the parable

Luke 15:13:

> *Not long after that, the younger son got together all he had, set off for a distant country and there squandered his wealth in wild living.*

While the request of the youngest son for his inheritance is completely lacking in respect, we see the father granting it without hesitation. The father does not deny him and does not try to change his mind. In contrast to the son, the father respects him. The father leaves him completely free in his choice, even if this choice is wrong.

After the son had received his share in the inheritance, it says that he 'got together all he had'. The inheritance wasn't a bag of money, it consisted of family possessions. It would have been lands, houses and cattle. Again, the son disregards all the values of their culture. You can't just sell all your family possessions; one simply does not do that. But he did, and that's how he procured a large sum of money.

But that is not all, he goes one step further. Instead of investing the money within the local community, he travels to a distant country and squanders his entire inheritance. In leaving home, the youngest son tries with all his might to become a 'non-son'. He wants to break all family ties. That's why he *left* his father's house, sold all he had, to try to start a new life in a *'distant country'*. Extremely determined he exercises his will and makes himself totally independent. He wants to define his own identity, and for this, he certainly doesn't want to be dependent on his father.

By his leaving the youngest son tries in all his strength to be a 'not-son'.

It is important to see that the father, throughout the entire process, gives the son *complete* freedom. The Father doesn't try to *overrule* his son's free will. Even though the son breaks the family tie, in his heart the father will always love him, the one who left the father's house and wants nothing to do with him or his family. This is how it is with all God's children!

With the pigs

Luke 15:15-19:

> So he went and hired himself out to a citizen of that country, who sent him to his fields to feed pigs. He longed to fill his stomach with the pods that the pigs were eating, but no one gave him anything. When he came to his senses, he said, 'How many of my father's hired servants have food to spare, and here I am starving to death! I will set out and go back to my father and say to him: Father, I have sinned against heaven and against you. I am no longer worthy to be called your son; make me like one of your hired servants.'

Here we see where the son's independence has led him. Looking at this from a negative perspective, we see he is in a place of hunger. He has no income or roof over his head; he is almost equal to pigs. But there is also a positive side to this situation. The father let him go so that he would discover and experience for himself exactly what independence has to offer him. And this the son has well and truly experienced, and it has brought him to the end of himself.

'My father'

This is the first time that the son thinks about the father as '*my* father' (emphasis mine)! The relationship he tried to get rid of has returned to his memory: my father . . . There is no intimacy yet, but deep down inside there is a desire for restoration, to go back – back home! What in fact has happened here, is that the son has come to a place where he lets himself be found.

Luke 15:20-21:

> So he got up and went to his father.
> 'But while he was still a long way off, his father saw him and was filled with compassion for him; he ran to his son, threw his arms round him and kissed him.
> The son said to him, 'Father, I have sinned against heaven and against you. I am no longer worthy to be called your son.'

This moment is often taken for the moment of conversion for the lost son. Earlier we noted that he already was a son when he left his father, otherwise he would have never received his share of the inheritance. His conversion is not his decision to head back home, the conversion is the choice he makes that brings him to the place where restoration with his father is possible. The conclusion

The conversion is the choice he makes that brings him to the place where restoration with his father is possible.

we can draw from this is that we, too, after our conversion, are not automatically in a place of intimacy with – and dependence on – the Father. We still have our own free will, the Father honours that. The great desire of the Father is to show us how much He loves us and how unconditional His love for us is.

The choice

Here the youngest son makes the right choice, but this doesn't change him. By distancing himself from his father and wanting to live independently of him, the son has placed himself in the position of 'being-orphaned'. The choice he makes to turn back to his father has not changed his mindset. His words *'I am no longer worthy to be called your son'* clearly tell us that he still thinks and lives out of being an orphan.

We can use our free will and choose to step out of dependence and intimacy with the Father. How to get back there is a different matter altogether. Dependency on the Father cannot be obtained through a decision we make! What the Father really says is: 'Come as you are. By showing you My unconditional love, you are getting to know Me as I really am, and who I want to be for you.'

Why does the father mention nothing of the mistakes his son has made? Why doesn't he tell him to ask for forgiveness first? Why does the father not reject him, and why does he show no intention of punishing the behaviour of his son?

We have learned that when you sin, there will be consequences, and so we also expect that from the Father. The son has sinned, he feels guilty and expects a fitting punishment from his father. How many of us have the exact same mindset as this son? It cannot be that the Father completely overlooks sin, can it?

It is therefore fundamental that we understand the heart of the Father. Why does He handle the way He does? To understand this is of great importance, because it greatly determines the image we have of God the Father!

The heart of the Father

We will take another look at the parable. The father is watching, waiting for the moment of his son's return. This shows the heart of a father longing for restoration, a father who longs to express his fatherhood. He then sees his son in the distance and it says that he was filled with compassion. To

Wounded people, wound people and healed people, heal people.

understand this more clearly, we will refer to the teachings of John and Paula Sandford. One of the things they highlight in their teaching is: *'wounded people, wound people and healed people, heal people.'* I think the father of the parable must also have been exposed to this teaching!

Let's take another look at what happens. The son has by his actions wounded the heart of the father. What effect has this when it happens to us? We are more often not very excited to embrace someone who has harmed us. Let them first show they are remorseful. Let him (or her) first prove that they are worth trusting again. In some cases, we even want nothing to do with them anymore. We build a wall around our heart, so that we don't get hurt again. We keep that person at a distance.

How different does the father respond here! Why doesn't he berate the son on his behaviour? We know, of course, from God the Father that there is forgiveness and grace. But does this mean you can do anything you want? Can you get away with absolutely everything? What do we experience when we come back to the Father? Do we feel guilty? What response do we expect from the Father?

(Time to reflect)

Muslim country

Let me begin by giving an illustration. Anneke and I were invited to a Muslim country somewhere in Asia. One evening we were speaking in one of the Christian churches in an area where Christians were allowed to live. We were in an upper room and the service started with worship. The worship was accompanied by a man at the front with a portable pipe organ. In this very small room around 120 men and women were sat on the floor.

When the worship ended, I was to get up to speak. I spoke that evening, as I often do, on the parable of the lost son. When I got to the part where the youngest son starts heading back home, I asked the question: 'Do you think he was afraid to see his father again?' Wholehearted and with one accord the entire room answered: 'Yes.' The answer was so resolute, that I decided to ask another question: 'When you sin, are you afraid of God?' Again, there came a definite 'yes' from the room. My question then was: 'But does this parable indicate that *he had to be* afraid of his father?'

(Time to reflect)

The Netherlands

The above example concerns people who have been raised and live in a Muslim country and culture. One thing is evident: there is always a fear of God. But what's it like in the Church in the Netherlands or in Western Europe? How often have we been spoken to from the pulpit with a raised finger: 'Watch out, otherwise God will . . . '? These experiences will largely determine the image we have of God the Father and it also determines the relationship we (want to) have with Him.

Fear and intimacy are direct opposites of each other. The moment we fear God the Father, we retreat to a considerable distance instead of longing for an intimate relationship with Him. But don't forget: God the Father has a fierce desire to share His heart completely with us. His desire for a restored relationship is even so big that He sent His only Son to die to make this possible.

The question

Did the lost son *trust* his father when he was on his way back home? Did he have the experience of being able to rely upon his father's love and acceptance? No, he did not. He wasn't counting on acceptance and being able to return as a son.

Luke 15:21:

> Then the son said to him, 'Father, I have sinned against heaven and before you; **I am no longer worthy to be called your son.'**

To be able to trust his father completely, it was necessary for him to first have the *experience* of his father completely trusting him. But how is it possible for the father to trust his son completely? His son had done virtually *nothing* to give his father the impression that he was trustworthy ...

The answer

We can see here that God the Father doesn't trust us based on what we have and haven't done, He trusts us because He is our Father! He knows us because He created us, and that is why He knows that from the moment we receive healing and are restored, we are trustworthy! By trusting us, the Father gives us the ability to, in turn, trust others. The same principle applies here that we read in 1 John about love:

1 John 4:19:

We love because he first loved us.

When we are His children, He wants to be our Father. He is not primarily concerned about our *doing*, but about our *being*.

And now continuing

It was only *after* the lost son had a personal revelation and experience of his father's trust in him that it became *possible* for the son to also trust his father. This is because he started to know his father for who he really was. This counts for us as well! Now we see that it has nothing to do with what we do or don't do or have done, but that the Father wants to bring us into a place of complete dependence.

John 1:12:

Yet to all who did receive him, to those who believed in his name, he gave the right to become children of God . . .

The image we have of God determines what He can do through us!

Only when a complete restoration of the relationship takes place can we have a right image of God the Father. Furthermore: the image we have of God determines what He can do through us!

(Time to reflect)

Tim: A modern parable

There is a story that I very much like to share. It is like a parable, not from the Bible, but from my own life. The story starts with my youngest son at the time when he is a little boy. We are living in an area where children play outside. There is a playground in the area, but to get there you must cross a busy road. Tim is three years old and I say to him: 'Tim, listen carefully, you are never to go to the playground on your own, do you understand that?' And Tim obediently answers me: 'Yes, Dad.'

But the day comes when the weather is nice, I am busy in the backyard and the front door is open. Tim walks out the front door, looks behind and sees that I am unaware of what he is doing. Determinedly, his little legs carry him in the direction of the playground. From a short distance the neighbour sees what is happening. Tim gets to the busy road and takes another look over his shoulder. No Daddy, that means cross! And Tim crosses the busy road, but he forgets to be careful. The car coming towards him, driving way too fast, tries to stop with all its might, screeching brakes, but hits little Tim and he flies through the air. With a smack he hits the road and lies there, motionless.

The neighbour stands frozen; what is he supposed to do? He immediately sees people rushing to the scene and calling emergency services on their cell phones. He decides to go to get me. The front door is still open and he runs in, shouting: 'Henk, you must come now! Tim has had an accident.'

Together we hurry to the place of the accident. We see a large group of people, and the police have already arrived. I hear the sirens of a nearby ambulance. 'Out of the way!' I yell to the people. 'I am his father!' The group of people moves aside and there I see Tim laying on the road, still motionless. I see that his eyes are open. Our eyes meet and I say: 'That's what you get, being disobedient! Do you hear that ambulance, it's coming for you! And when you come out of the hospital you can expect a fierce punishment from me!'

Do you think I responded like that? No, of course not! I kneel right beside Tim, and I put my arm around him. I can't pick him up because I don't know if his neck or spine is damaged. But I want to reassure him that I'm there, and I tell him: 'I will stay with you, Tim, it's going to be all right, I love you!'

Do you believe He is there for you, and that He, filled with compassion, takes you in his arms ... ?

We find it totally acceptable when a father responds this way. Of course Tim will not be punished. Tim has truly experienced the consequences of his disobedience. What he needs now is a father who is there for him. But what is our image of God, when we have sinned? Do you believe He is there for you, and that He, filled with compassion, takes you into his arms and says: 'I am your Father, I will care for you'? Or do we believe He stands ready to accuse us with His prying finger, and says: 'When you have sinned you know the consequences...'?

The homecoming

Luke 15:20:

But while he was still a long way off, his father saw him and was filled with compassion for him; he ran to his son, threw his arms round him and kissed him.

The father sees his son appear. All the father's feelings of pain and hurt start to surface. He feels the pain in his heart again. But instead of focusing on the pain and acting in response to it, he chooses to use his pain as fuel for his love. The father realises that the hurt from his son comes from a wounded heart. A wounded heart will always bring forth bad things. It is the heart of an *orphan*. And the father knows that the one thing that is needed now is the healing of his son's wounded heart. And full of compassion he embraces his son and kisses him.

What foolishness to think that God would say to an orphan: 'You need to try harder! I am expecting different behaviour from you now!' No, from the very beginning it was within the Father's heart to say: 'Come as you are. Come into that place where you let yourself be found. And I will be there. I will take you in My arms and fill your heart with My love. That is how you will know that I am your Father, and that you are My son, My daughter.'

The restoration of sonship

Luke 15:22-24:

> But the father said to his servants, 'Quick! Bring the best robe and put it on him. Put a ring on his finger and sandals on his feet. Bring the fattened calf and kill it. Let's have a feast and celebrate. For this son of mine was dead and is alive again; he was lost and is found.' So they began to celebrate.

Here we see in a beautiful way how the father operates. God's plan is completely focused on restoration. From sonship it is possible to live out the destiny He intended for you!

Kenneth E. Bailey describes this beautifully in his book, *The Cross & the Prodigal.* He says: 'First, the father gives **himself** to his 'lost' son! Second, he welcomes **the son** back into the family, so that he can be restored to the place he belongs again.' (Emphasis: author's.)

Welcome home!

Time to reflect:

What image of God the Father do you have? Can you believe that He loves you as you are? Take the time to let this really sink in. Try to position yourself in a place where you *let* yourself be found by the Father. Every day He longs for you with intense desire!

To listen:

Julie True, 'Heaven's Embrace' (spontaneous song)

Additional reading:

Jack Winter, *The Homecoming* (Edmonds, WA: YWAM Publishing, 1999)

Kenneth E. Bailey, *The Cross & the Prodigal* (Downers Grove, IL: IVP, 2005)

John and Paula Sandford, *The Transformation of the Inner Man* (Tulsa, OK: Victory House, 1982)

Space for notes/reflections:

FIVE

The Five Wise and the Five Foolish Virgins and other parables

Matthew 24:45-46 (*The Message*):

Who here qualifies for the job of overseeing the kitchen? A person the Master can depend on to feed the workers on time each day. Someone the Master can drop in on unannounced and always find him doing his job.

Hearing God's voice

What you have just read can have a big effect on how you view yourself as a Christian. God the Father's intention is not that we join or confess a Christian religion, but that we grow in an intimate relationship with Him. When we carefully read the Bible, we can discover God's plan for our lives. By this, however, I do not mean that you must become a Bible scholar to discover His plans for you.

I sometimes pose the question: 'Is it important to hear God's voice?' The answer I always get is: 'Yes, of course!' Then I ask: 'What is even more important than hearing God's voice?' This usually sparks a few different answers but one will often stand out: 'Obedience!' Personally, I think there is something even more important than that. And that is to know the One who is speaking ...

Parables

Jesus often speaks to the people in parables. He does this so that they will understand that which is otherwise difficult to hear. Nevertheless, it is good to take into consideration that when you have a wrong image of God, you can also wrongly interpret His words. This can also happen with Jesus' parables.

In the Gospel of Matthew, we read the parable of the wise and the foolish virgins.

Matthew 25:1-2:

At that time the kingdom of heaven will be like ten virgins who took their lamps and went out to meet the bridegroom. Five of them were foolish and five were wise.

Let's begin by asking ourselves some questions about this parable. What do you think, did the foolish virgins know they were foolish when they went out? I don't think so. Did they know that amongst them there were five wise virgins? I don't think so either.

Now let's look at the wise virgins. Do you think they had the foresight and knowledge from the beginning that there were five foolish virgins amongst them? Probably not. That leaves us with one final question: did the wise virgins know when they went out that they were different, that they belonged to the group of the five wise virgins? I highly doubt it!

The purpose of the parable

Jesus obviously shares this parable with a purpose. It is therefore important to know what kind of analogy He is drawing. For example, who or what is He signifying with these ten virgins? Could it be that He is talking about the Church, about the congregation? If that is the case, could it be that with this parable He is highlighting the fact that in the Church, there are both wise and foolish believers?

(Time to reflect)

Testimony

Whenever I speak on this parable (and the one about the talents), I've noticed that there are always a few people who get nervous. Their worry is that they are unsure if they belong to the group of wise virgins.

Quite some time after I had been speaking on a boat conference in Germany, I heard a testimony. One of the people on board had a leading role in their church. During this conference, I had spoken about this parable of the five wise and five foolish virgins. This person had mentioned to a friend that whenever he heard this parable, the following thought came to mind: 'How can I be absolutely certain that I am not part of the foolish virgins?' Even though he had been a Christian for a long time, it still made him doubt. The explanation he got while he was on board, however, put him at ease, and he was very glad he got it. He told me that rest had entered his heart. He was now certain, knowing without a doubt that he was part of the wise virgins! When he got home he told his wife about this new-found rest. A few months later he suddenly passed away, but he did so with the assurance he had so longed for.

Entering in or staying outside

It is interesting to discover what message Jesus has for the Church in this parable. I Don't believe it is just 'interesting' for us, it is extremely important. What is being concluded at the end of this parable is that there are five who enter in with the bridegroom, and five that stay outside.

Matthew 25:1-8:

> At that time the kingdom of heaven will be like ten virgins who took their lamps and went out to meet the bridegroom. Five of them were foolish and five were wise. The foolish ones took their lamps but did not take any oil with them. The wise ones, however, took oil in jars along with their lamps. The bridegroom was a long time in coming, and they all became drowsy and fell asleep. At midnight the cry rang out: 'Here's the bridegroom! Come out to meet him!' Then all the virgins woke up and trimmed their lamps. The foolish ones said to the wise, 'Give us some of your oil; our lamps are going out.'

Let's assume that we can apply this parable to a group of believers. I believe we can, because we see that all ten virgins knew that the coming of the bridegroom was imminent. We also see that all ten of them had taken a burning lamp. This we know, because the scripture says: 'Give us some of your oil; our lamps are going out.'

Knowing that the lamps were burning reveals that the foolish virgins had oil in their lamps to begin with. The only difference is that the five wise virgins had taken with them *extra* oil in a jar. The foolish ones did not. This turns out to be a matter of vital importance, because it is the only difference that determines who can enter in, and who does not get access to the wedding feast.

Matthew 25:11-12:

Later the others also came. 'Lord, Lord,' they said, 'open the door for us!' But he replied, 'Truly I tell you, I don't know you.'

The oil

The oil, or the lack thereof, is the central issue in this parable. It is therefore important to understand what Jesus is signifying here. What is 'oil' representative of in the Bible? Very often it symbolises the Holy Spirit. But I don't think it has the same meaning here, because the foolish virgins also had oil, perhaps no extra oil, but they did have it. It cannot be that when we arrive at the wedding feast, we will be told: 'Too bad, I am very sorry, but you didn't have enough Holy Spirit. Sorry!'

What then, could this extra oil be representative of?

I once heard John Arnott, a pastor from Canada, preach on this; he said that we must look at the clue that is given at the very end of the parable. Here the Lord says: 'I don't know you.' The fact that the other virgins were allowed to enter in earlier that night, shows that they did know Him. We can conclude from this parable that having a relationship with the Father and being known by Him is something entirely different than just believing that He exists.

The Father says: 'It doesn't really touch My heart when you only visit church once a week, or maybe even go to a Bible study. I long to be part of your life, to be close to you and let you know how much I love you. I want to reveal My Father's heart to you.' Considering this thought, I think the extra oil represents a true relationship, having real intimacy with the Father!

Having a relationship with the Father and being known by Him is something entirely different than just believing that He exists.

Later in this chapter I will go deeper into the meaning of this parable, there is much more to discover. But first, I want to look at the parable that follows directly after this one. This parable does not stand on its own. What Jesus is talking about here is part of a larger picture. The next parable is the one of the talents.

The parable of the talents

In this parable, we see Jesus giving an example of three people who are given an assignment, and how they respond to this.

Matthew 25:14-15:

> *Again, it will be like a man going on a journey, who called his servants and entrusted his wealth to them. To one he gave five bags of gold, to another two bags, and to another one bag, each according to his ability. Then he went on his journey.*

We see here that there are slaves or servants who attempt to achieve something and are rewarded. And we see one who gets a single talent doesn't use it, and therefore comes under judgement.

Matthew 25:26-30:

> *His master replied, 'You wicked, lazy servant! So you knew that I harvest where I have not sown and gather where I*

have not scattered seed? Well then, you should have put my money on deposit with the bankers, so that when I returned I would have received it back with interest. So take the bag of gold from him and give it to the one who has ten bags. For whoever has will be given more, and they will have an abundance. Whoever does not have, even what they have will be taken from them. And throw that worthless servant outside, into the darkness, where there will be weeping and gnashing of teeth.'

Where is the loving father in these parables?

When I read these two parables I was faced with a big problem. For so many years I have solely spoken on the revelation of the Father heart of God, about the infinite love of the Father. But where is His love, His compassion for the sinner in these parables?

I simply did not believe that what I was reading could be true. But now I had a problem, because there it is, written in the Bible, and the Word of God is always truth, isn't it? Nevertheless, I couldn't leave it at this. The Father I had come to know simply did not belong in the picture being painted by these parables.

We read in this parable and in the words of the wise and foolish virgins, about those that 'do right' and are rewarded, and about others who 'do wrong' and are consequently excluded. We see slaves or servants who attempt to achieve something and are rewarded. And we see someone who gets a single talent, doesn't use it, and comes under judgement because of it.

I have always read these parables as an example given by Jesus of how things will be when He returns. But if that is true, where do we find the compassion for the lost? Where

Where is His love, His compassion for the sinner in these parables?

is that heart filled with love that reaches out to the sinner, and where are the open arms of the Father welcoming home His lost son?

I've noticed many people who read these parables questioning themselves: 'Am I doing well enough?' It cannot be the Father's intention to use a form of fear to make sure we do enough for Him. Be careful: when we simply accept what we read here, we are the same as the lazy servant! We then have the same image of God, a ruthless God, who gives you what you deserve!

How can we reconcile this with, for example, the following Bible verses?

Ezekiel 18:23:

> **Do I take any pleasure in the death of the wicked?** *declares the Sovereign Lord.*

John 3:16:

> *For God so loved* **the world** *that he gave his one and only Son, that whoever believes in him shall not perish but have eternal life.*

Luke 15:

> **The lost son . . .**

1 John 4:8:

> *Whoever does not love does not know God,* **because God is love.**

He is unchangeable, isn't He, always the same?

The image of God

I started this chapter by saying how important it is to know the One who is speaking. Through the years, I have come to know God the Father as a loving Father, so in these parables I look to discover the heart of a loving Father. I don't settle for anything less! There is also an important consequence that is determined by the image we have of God.

Adam and Eve

If there ever were people, apart from Jesus, who had a good image of God, it would have been Adam and Eve. We read that He spoke with them and came and walked with them in 'the cool of the day' (Genesis 3:8). And yet, we read that they were afraid when God addresses them after they had sinned.

Genesis 3:10:

> He answered, 'I heard you in the garden, and I was afraid because I was naked; so I hid.'

That is strange. Do you think there was any time before the Fall that they feared God? Absolutely not! Did God change because of the Fall? Certainly not! That leaves us with only one possible conclusion: the image they had of God was changed through sin! And moreover, it also influenced their self-image. As said before, the image we have of God determines what He can do through us! Sin changes our image of God.

Returning to the parables

We can read these parables and make the conclusion that God passes judgement on those who have done wrong, and that you must try your very best that you might be spared . . .

The image we have of God determines what He can do through us!

But is the only purpose of these parables to emphasise the issue of judgement? Isn't it weird, to say the least, that Jesus doesn't offer a solution, only judgement? Shouldn't a parable of the kingdom carry a message of hope within itself? Isn't it the purpose of a parable to signify something, so that the listener can better their life?

You can certainly read this parable as a warning. But what is the solution? Is it only when you work hard and try your best that you get the reward? How does this relate to what we have previously learned; that the Father wants us to be dependent on Him and that grace has nothing to do with our own effort? What happened to my loving Father?

I don't believe that the warning you read in these verses is the one and final purpose that Jesus had in speaking these parables. Wouldn't the purpose be that through the warning something changes for the better? Isn't that the heart of God?

Jonah

A good example of change for the better can be seen in the story of Jonah, who was sent to Nineveh. God sees a city heading for judgement. This is something close to His heart, and so He is looking for a way to avert judgement. He selects Jonah to warn the inhabitants of Nineveh. Jonah initially has no desire to get involved in this matter, but after a peculiar intervention of God, he 'freely' decides to bring the message to Nineveh. After having delivered his message, he waits on a hill outside the city for the judgement of God to be executed. But no judgement comes!

Why is there no judgement? Because Jonah revealed God to the inhabitants of Nineveh and the people repented. In the Gospels of Matthew and Luke, Jesus even compares Himself to Jonah.

Matthew 12:40-41:

*For as Jonah was three days and three nights in the belly of a huge fish, so the Son of Man will be three days and three nights in the heart of the earth. 41 The men of Nineveh will stand up at the judgment with this generation and condemn it; for they repented at the preaching of Jonah, **and now something greater than Jonah is here**.*

Luke 11:30:

*For as Jonah was a sign to the Ninevites, **so also will the Son of Man be to this generation**.*

We read here that Jesus Himself wants to prevent people from coming under judgement. He wants to warn them, that's exactly what's in His heart. And we know that what's in Jesus' heart has come straight from the heart of the Father!

What, then, is the purpose of these parables?

Let's look at the context in which Jesus is speaking these parables. Who is He predominantly speaking to here? Whenever I ask this question, most people think that He is either speaking to the multitude, or the Pharisees and Sadducees of the day. Neither is the case. It all starts a chapter earlier when Jesus is on the Mount of Olives and the disciples come

No judgement comes!

to Him. After one of them asks a question, He starts telling them what is going to happen.

Matthew 24:3:

> As Jesus was sitting on the Mount of Olives, **the disciples came to him privately**. 'Tell us,' they said, 'when will this happen, and what will be the sign of your coming and of the end of the age?'

He privately speaks to His disciples about the things that are going to happen and He paints, as it were, a picture of what it will look like. So, Jesus is on the Mount of Olives and speaks these parables to them, not to the 'multitude', and not to the Pharisees and Sadducees. But why is He specifically speaking these parables to the disciples? Does He believe they have a wrong image of God? I don't think that is the case.

John 14:9:

> Anyone who has seen me has seen the Father. How can you say, 'Show us the Father'?

The disciples spent three years with Jesus. Was there ever a group of people who got to know Him and the Father better? I doubt it. With the exception of Judas, we can conclude with a high probability that He does not count His disciples among the five foolish virgins, or sees them as a servant who doesn't use the talent they've been given. But why does He speak these parables to His disciples, when really, He wants to reach a different group of people?

A different perspective

One day, when I was pondering this question, I suddenly saw what God the Father wanted to communicate with these parables. He wants to point out that the image that the man with the single talent has of God, *it's not right*! Jesus doesn't emphasise the fact that he is doing wrong which leads to punishment. Jesus is showing us why he is doing wrong. This is what He is communicating to His disciples!

The question, therefore, is: why are the foolish virgins foolish, and why has the one with the single talent done wrong? He is not highlighting people's shortcomings in these parables but, full of compassion, He is painting a picture showing us what we miss out on when we have a wrong image of God. He describes what life looks like when we have no intimacy with the Father.

The challenge

The challenge Jesus puts before His disciples is the same challenge God gave to Jonah. The parables were meant to awaken compassion in the hearts of the disciples. Jesus is showing them what, in fact, will take place. There are probably so many in the churches who have one talent. Only a few who have five talents. Therefore, those who have one talent form a large group, they

Full of compassion, He is painting a picture showing us what we miss out on when we have a wrong image of God.

are important. Just like the five foolish virgins, it is a group of people dear to the Father's heart.

Jesus says: 'See what happens when people don't have the right image of the Father. See what position they find themselves in when they hear: "I did not know you."'

The challenge does not primarily pertain to those who are doing the wrong, but Jesus lays the challenge before

His disciples. He hands *them* the task of telling the people about the Father so that they will get to know Him for who He really is! Through these parables, He is warning the disciples. He says: 'Look what happens when they get a wrong image of God, a wrong image of the Father . . .'

Right before Jesus speaks these parables to His disciples, He says something else:

Matthew 24:45-47:

> *Who here qualifies for the job of overseeing the kitchen? A person the Master can depend on to feed the workers on time each day. Someone the Master can drop in on unannounced and always find him doing his job.*

Now I recognise the heart of the Father again in these parables!

This text has been taken from *The Message* translation by Eugene Petersen, which you read at the beginning of this chapter. This is what Jesus wants to communicate through these parables. He is saying: 'Do you see how important it is that the right image of God the Father is restored!?' And we get to carry this revelation. We need pioneers who have the right image of God the Father and can reveal Him to the Church!

These parables tell us that without the right image of the Father, you cannot enter into the place God has for you. Now I recognise the heart of the Father in these parables!

Jeremiah 31:3 (*The Message*):

> *God told them, 'I've never quit loving you and never will. Expect love, love, and more love!*

Time to reflect:

When you realise that you don't yet know the Father in intimacy, do not be afraid. He longs for this relationship more than you. Talk to Him, tell Him: 'Father, I want to know You better.' Take the time to experience His presence.

To listen:

Paul Baloche, 'My Hope'

Additional reading:

Wayne Jacobsen, *He Loves Me!* (Nashville, TN: FaithWords, 2008)

Space for notes/reflections:

SIX

The Lost Sheep

Galatians 5:1 (*The Message*):

Christ has set us free to live a free life.
So take your stand! Never again let
anyone put a harness of slavery on you.

Another parable

In the previous chapters, we extensively looked at the parable of the lost son, and we will spend some more time on this yet. But as I noted earlier, these parables are part of a series of three, and they consistently speak of something that was lost and then is found again. In the first parable Jesus speaks to us about a lost sheep.

Luke 15:1-6:

> *Now the tax collectors and sinners were all gathering round to hear Jesus. But the Pharisees and the teachers of the law muttered, 'This man welcomes sinners, and eats with them.' Then Jesus told them this parable: 'Suppose one of you has a hundred sheep and loses one of them. Doesn't he leave the ninety-nine in the open country and go after the lost sheep until he finds it? And when he finds it, he joyfully puts it on his shoulders and goes home. Then he calls his friends and neighbours together and says, 'Rejoice with me; I have found my lost sheep.'*

We see here that Jesus has a mixed audience of listeners. First there are the sinners, who love to come and listen to Him, and of course the Pharisees and teachers of the law who often try to catch Him out. In this parable, Jesus speaks of Himself. He is the shepherd in this story. In fact, He brings to life Psalm 23.

Psalm 23:1-6:

> *The Lord is my shepherd, I lack nothing. He makes me lie down in green pastures, he leads me beside quiet waters, he refreshes my soul. He guides me along the right paths for his name's sake. Even though I walk through the darkest valley, I will fear no evil, for you are with me; your rod and your staff, they comfort me. You prepare a table before me in the presence of my enemies. You anoint my head with oil; my cup overflows. Surely your goodness and love will follow me all the days of my life, and I will dwell in the house of the Lord for ever.*

The tax collectors and sinners love to hear Him speak like this. But the Pharisees and teachers of the law aren't impressed. And predominantly to *them,* Jesus turns to this parable (or parables). And while He speaks the words: 'Suppose one of you has a hundred sheep . . .' He watches the Pharisees and teachers of the law. Ouch, that hurts. I am a teacher of the law, a Pharisee, I am important, I'm not a shepherd. (A shepherd in these days was not a high position by any social standards.) Oh well, what's He saying now? I own 100 sheep? Oh, I am the owner, so that means I am rich. OK, I can live with that, continue . . .

Luke 15:4:

Suppose one of you has a hundred sheep and loses one of them. Doesn't he leave the ninety-nine in the open country and go after the lost sheep until he finds it?

Hey, hang on, that's not how it should go. Do you even know who I am? I will get my servant to go and find the sheep. There is no way I am doing that myself! Meanwhile the tax collector and sinners are gloating. *Yes*, good one, beautiful, go on!

Kenneth E. Bailey says in his book *The Cross & the Prodigal* that people in those days, in that culture never blamed themselves. That was simply inconceivable. When someone would miss the train, they would not say: 'I have missed the train', but 'The train has passed me . . .'[2] Jesus went against all the customs and traditions of their language by saying: 'When he had lost one . . .' What Jesus in fact was saying to the teachers of the law and the Pharisees, was this: 'Do you even realise that you are the ones who have lost your "sheep"? I am the One that will go after them and I will bring them home and now you have the audacity to come and complain to Me? Don't you understand that I am correcting *your* mistakes?'

The shepherd did leave the ninety-nine other sheep in the wilderness to go and find the one. Was that a good move? What is more important? To find the lost one, or care for the rest of the flock so that nothing happens to them? You can imagine the sheep talking to each other: 'What is he going to do? Is he leaving us here to fend for ourselves? I am afraid, what if something happens to us!?'

But then there's one that says: 'Listen here, if he doesn't go and find that lost one, that means there's only ninety-

---

2. Kenneth E Bailey, *The Cross & The Prodigal* (Downers Grove, IL: IVP, 2000), p. 151.

nine of us left. And what happens next time someone goes missing, and after that? The group will get smaller and smaller. What if I am the one who makes a mistake next time, and goes missing? Now that I see he will look for that lost one, I know he will also look for me until he has found me. That is why it gives me more rest and security to see him go than if he stayed with us.'

If the shepherd had chosen the group over the individual, everyone would have eventually started to feel insecure. When something happens to you, you won't be important enough, and you will be left behind. But now the entire group has been put at ease. They know every individual matters and is important enough to be rescued, cared for and brought home. Beautiful! The one is important to the shepherd!

Behind the wall

One Sunday evening after the service, at our VaderHuis church, someone I knew approached me. He said: 'Do you have a moment?' I said: 'Of course.' He continued: 'I realise that over time, I have built walls around my heart, and I think it would be good to break these down. Would you pray with me?' Naturally, I was prepared to help, and I was about to start praying when God suddenly spoke to me. I got a sense that He was saying: 'Tell him that he doesn't have to break down his walls.'

This came as a complete surprise. Like so many of us in pastoral leadership, we have learned that we must break down the walls we ourselves built. These walls create blockages between people, but also between us and God. I assumed that God was aware of this, so I asked Him: 'What do I say, then . . . ?'

Again, I got the sense that God asked me: 'Will you tell him that he doesn't have to break down his walls?' 'Yes, but . . . what do I say?' Again, I got the sense of God asking me: 'Will you tell him?' and I felt it was the last time He would ask. I wasn't sure what to do. If I decided to tell him he didn't have to break down his walls, and he asked me: 'Oh really, why not?', I would be at a loss for words. But saying nothing wasn't an option either.

I then had a bright idea. It was something we learned in Youth With a Mission. Instead of saying: 'Thus saith the Lord . . .' it was better to say: 'I get the sense that God is saying . . .' So that's what I did. (All this happened in a few seconds.) I said: 'I think God wants to tell you that you don't have to break down your walls.'

Directly after came, as it were, a *download* from God, and I was able to continue speaking. The Father said: 'My son, I know you have built walls, you did this with a reason. I am not asking you to break down your walls. What I am asking is: will you allow Me to come in behind your walls, so that I can be with you? I want to be there for you and hold you in my arms. I want to do this until you experience from Me, the safety you experienced before from the wall. Only then will I help you to stand, but you can keep the wall, for I am taking a new direction with you. And if at any point you feel the need to hide behind the wall, you may. I know why you built that wall in the first place! But know that when you go to the wall to hide, I will always be there with you.'

(Time to reflect)

Wow, I myself was blown away by this. It changed for a large part the way I look at pastoral leadership and it changed (again) my image of God. What a loving Father He is! I realised that very often we have learned that God expects us to do something, and that He will respond to that. But that is almost the same as: 'When you try your best, I will reward you for that.' While grace teaches us that it is an unconditional gift! But now it gets interesting, because in what other areas of our lives is this transformed image of God having a new effect...?

Back to the lost sheep

Let's try to understand how all this applies to the lost sheep. She is in a tight spot; her coat is stuck in a thorny bush. She has been left behind because she went away from the flock. She was so set on going her own way. And there she is, stuck in the bushes, an easy prey for any wild animal and not able to get herself home. She's afraid.

The one is important to the shepherd!

But then the sheep hears someone calling in the distance, and she thinks: 'Someone is calling my name! It's the shepherd! He noticed I went missing! He has been looking for me! Baaaaaah, I am here! He has found me! He has freed me from the thorny bush and dressed my wounds! He even put me on his strong shoulders and carried me all the way home...'

The lost sheep in this parable symbolises a sinner who comes to repentance. But there is something peculiar about this: it doesn't appear to be a very dramatic conversion. Isn't it expected at a conversion to be repentant, or that you confess all the things you have done wrong? Nothing of the sort is the case here. And not only here, with the lost sheep, but also not with the lost coin or the lost son! What we are witnessing here is the working of grace, God's unconditional gift.

Revelation through experience

What happens here, is that the lost sheep is receiving an abundance of grace and love, without having to do anything for it. We see that the shepherd does *everything*. He first discovered that his sheep went missing, then he himself went out looking for her. He didn't send a hired hand, saying: 'Listen here, I lost one of my sheep, you go and look for her!' He went out to look for her and found her, he then dressed her wounds and said: 'I don't think you will be able to get home on your own. Come, let me carry you.' That is how he, carrying her on his shoulders, brought the lost sheep back home.

It is incredibly important to the Father that He can show you, in practice, that you *can* be *totally* dependent on Him. The best way to get to know Him like this, is to experience Him personally. This is revelation through experience.

When you go to the wall to hide, I will always be there with you.

Repentance

How does Jesus look at repentance? It is actually quite simple. Jesus defines repentance as allowing yourself to be found. Repentance means to Jesus, that you position yourself to where you let yourself be found by the Father. In knowing this, restoration of the dependency on God becomes even more pivotal. You then say: 'I give up, I cannot do it myself; everything I have, all that I am, belongs to You!'

And here is the crux: in the process of restoration, while you are already receiving the love of the Father, comes out of the heart a deep repentance. Love and restoration do not come to you *because or after* you have repented and showed that you are remorseful!

Love and restoration do not come to you *because or after* you have repented ... The big difference here is that repentance follows on the total acceptance of who you *are*, and even more than that; the Father gives you His unconditional love, even before you have done anything to deserve it. This touches something deep in us. Here is a response to that unconditional love. When you (re-)experience repentance like this, you will want to approach everything from the love you have for Him, instead of working to earn His love.

Even one step further

Through this parable, we have received revelation on the Father heart of God. The deep desire of the Father is that His children who are still in the world also get the opportunity to see and know Him for who He really is.

We see in this parable that the Father does not operate under the principle of 'if you, then you'. He gives His love without saying: 'Now I want you to be repentant.' He doesn't expect anything in return, and that is precisely the essence of *agape* love. A love that is freely given! Are we able, filled with this *agape* love of the Father, to love others the same way?

Would we love a Muslim, without expecting them to be repentant, to simply show them that God the Father loves them as they are?

Yapton Free Church

One time Anneke and I were in England, in Yapton. We were at a Father heart conference and spoke on this parable, on how the lost sheep was found. On the Sunday, a lady who was almost eighty came to Anneke. She said to her: 'My entire life I have been searching for the Father, and yesterday, He found *me*!' This is why it is so important to come to that place where you *let* yourself be found, and so come into intimacy with your heavenly Father. Nothing can replace intimacy with the Father!

What we are witnessing here is the working of grace, God's unconditional gift.

Time to reflect:

How amazing it is that the Father doesn't start with what you have to do, but that He says: 'Let Me come to you first.' Today, can you come to that place where you *let* yourself be found?

To listen:

Julie True, 'Healing in Your Presence' from *Find Rest: Live Soaking Worship Music* (www.julietrue.com)

Additional reading:

Mark Stibbe, *The Father You've Been Waiting For* (Milton Keynes: Authentic, 2006)

Space for notes/reflections:

SEVEN

The Orphan

John 14:18:

I will not leave you as orphans;
I will come to you.

Intimacy and identity

In this chapter, we will look at where Adam and Eve ended up after the Fall and what consequences this had for them; and for us!

From the beginning, God had a purpose for mankind. God wanted every human being to fully walk in their destiny. And for this destiny, Adam and Eve received their identity from the Father, an identity that makes it possible to live as a son or daughter of Him. You cannot develop this identity yourself, you are dependent on God the Father for it. Receiving it while being at a distance is not possible either, it is in intimacy with Him where the Father gives you the identity of *sonship*. Through *intimacy*, you receive your *identity* and this is how you can reach your *destiny*.

It is important for us to realise that being a child of God is not the same as living in sonship. Living in sonship is the destination, becoming a child of God by becoming a Christian is how we reach our destination.

In other words: it is possible to be a child of God and still not live in sonship. Sonship is about our relationship with

Jesus; both men and women can receive it, and by it, as son or daughter, they can live in and from their destiny.

Your dependency on God and receiving your identity are no isolated events, like for example, choosing to receive this at your conversion. It is a process belonging to a lifestyle. It is best explained like this: you move from a workplace to a resting place. This is how Jesus lived His life!

John 5:19:

> Jesus gave them this answer: 'Very truly I tell you, the Son can do nothing by himself; he can do only what he sees his Father doing, because whatever the Father does the Son also does.

At the Fall, Adam and Eve separated themselves from God, their Father. They were still children of God, but it was no longer possible for them to live in *sonship*. They became orphans. After Adam and Eve, the entire creation was separated from God through sin, effectively placing the entire creation in the position of *'being-orphaned'*.

The definition of an orphan

An orphan to me is this: a child that has been cut off from parental care and has not been adopted. We see that the lost son made the same choice as Adam and Eve. He wanted no longer to be dependent on his father. He wanted to go his own way. He separated himself from his father and as a result was no longer able to live in sonship, effectively making himself an orphan.

When we look to Jesus, on the other hand, we see that He chooses to be completely dependent on the Father. That is how He could reach His final destination. Jesus walked and lived in and from a place of sonship.

When you have become a child of God, it does not automatically mean that you live out your sonship actively. After you became a Christian, the way to the Father was opened, and it was made possible to come into intimacy with Him. In this position, you are able to receive from Him the identity of sonship. Do you remember when Jesus said: 'I am the gate'? He also says: 'I am the way' (John 10:9; John 14:6). He invites us to use the opportunity He has given us, to start on the way to the Father.

The lost son became repentant when he was with the pigs and realised that he had nothing left. There, he thought of his father for the first time. He had done all he could to be independent. He didn't want to be dependent on his father for his identity, he wanted to create his own identity. He comes to the realisation that he's not going to make it, he remembers home, and his father.

Luke 15:14-17:

After he had spent everything, there was a severe famine in that whole country, and he began to be in need. So he went and hired himself out to a citizen of that country, who sent him to his fields to feed pigs. He longed to fill his stomach with the pods that the pigs were eating, but no one gave him anything. When he came to his senses, he said, 'How many of my father's hired servants have food to spare, and here I am starving to death!

The turning point

This is a turning point in his life. However, it is important to recognise that despite this decision, he is unable to change himself. He recalls the way he left home. Can he still go home? Is it possible to repair all the damage he has done? Is he even allowed to return?

Luke 15:18-19:

> *I will set out and go back to my father and say to him:*
> *Father, I have sinned against heaven and against you.*
> ***I am no longer worthy to be called your son;*** *make me*
> *like one of your hired servants.*

He then decides to take the risk and on the way home, he rehearses what he will say to his father. This part is important, because it reveals to us the way the youngest son thinks. We see him making the right decision by going home, but at the same time, we also see that he is unable to return to the position of sonship in his own strength. He says: 'I am no longer worthy to be called your son . . .' He is on the way home, but he (still) has the mindset of an orphan.

We can, after becoming a Christian, still make choices using our own free will. Would we dare to trust our Father so much that we would use our free will to give up our independence? Just like Adam and Eve and the lost son, we can choose our independence over connection and intimacy with the Father. We can use our free will and decide to step out of intimacy with Him, but we must realise that only through total dependence is it possible to come into an intimate relationship with God the Father.

Luke 15:20-24:

> *So he got up and went to his father. But while he was still*
> *a long way off, his father saw him and was filled with*
> *compassion for him; he ran to his son, threw his arms*
> *round him and kissed him. The son said to him, 'Father,*
> *I have sinned against heaven and against you. I am*
> *no longer worthy to be called your son.' But the father*
> *said to his servants, 'Quick! Bring the best robe and*

put it on him. Put a ring on his finger and sandals on his feet. Bring the fattened calf and kill it. Let's have a feast and celebrate. For this son of mine was dead and is alive again; he was lost and is found.' So they began to celebrate.

The homecoming

The good news is that the son was never absent from his father's heart, even though he had tried everything to stay as far away as possible from his father. You would expect the father to first let his son grovel in the dirt. To let him feel how wrong he was. Let him be uncertain for a while if he really is allowed to come home. Or tell him to first take a bath and get changed, and then we will talk, because he stinks! Nothing of the sort happens. The father runs to him and makes no mention of the things his son has done wrong. He doesn't listen to his excuses, but takes his son without any hesitation in his arms and passionately kisses him.

How is this possible? What is Jesus saying here? What image is he showing us here of God the Father? Can you sin without there being any consequences? Can you do whatever you want, because when you come to the Father, He will say to you: 'It doesn't matter, I love you anyway'? This doesn't seem to be right, but it is what the parable is showing. How does this really work?

(Time to reflect)

Extreme grace

To understand the attitude of the father I want to explain a principle of God that has to do with grace. There are people who say: 'Whatever you do, there is always grace, so you are free to do what you want.' Let me first ask a question: 'Is the love of God unconditional?' The answer is, of course, 'Yes.' The second question is: 'Is there always enough grace and does God always want to extend forgiveness?' Often this is where concerns start to arise. They say to me: 'Yes, God always wants to forgive, but you do have to ask for it' or 'but you have to be really sorry' or 'but you do have to be become a Christian'.

Charles R. Swindoll cites in his book *The Grace Awakening*, Martin Lloyd-Jones[3] who once said, and I paraphrase: 'If you think you are really preaching grace, yet no one is taking advantage of it, maybe you haven't preached it hard enough or strong enough.'

(Time to reflect)

It is a real dilemma. Of course, God's love is unconditional and His grace is limitless. But you can't just do whatever you want, can you? That's not right, is it? But how do you deal with the fact that there are people who 'abuse' grace and say: 'What I do doesn't really matter anymore, for even through all my mistakes it will be revealed how big God's grace is.' Paul wrote about this very issue in his letter to the Romans.

Through *intimacy*, you receive your *identity* and this is how you can reach your *destiny*.

Romans 6:1-4:

*What shall we say, then? Shall we go on sinning, **so that grace may increase?** By no means! We are those who*

---

3. Charles R. Swindoll, *The Grace Awakening* (Nashville, TN: Thomas Nelson, 2012), chapter 3, p. 35: Martin Lloyd-Jones, *Romans* (Carlisle, PA: The Banner of Truth Trust, 1986).

have died to sin; how can we live in it any longer? Or don't you know that all of us who were baptised into Christ Jesus were baptised into his death? We were therefore buried with him through baptism into death in order that, just as Christ was raised from the dead through the glory of the Father, **we too may live a new life.**

Again, the question: 'Can an orphan sin and does he need forgiveness and grace?' I always get a clear response: 'Yes, of course.' The next question is: 'Can a son (or daughter) sin and does he (or she) *also* need forgiveness and grace? Here too, I generally get the answer: 'Yes, of course!'

This tells us that concerning this issue there is no difference between an orphan and someone living in sonship. We all need the same grace from God! But what does an orphan become when he receives grace? Some will say: 'He will become a son.' But that is not true. An orphan who receives grace is a *forgiven orphan.* As an orphan, you can do good and bad things, but as a son you can also do good and bad things. When we are focused on the *doing,* it should be that doing good in both cases brings forth good fruit. There is however, a huge difference in *doing good* and *being good*! Religion teaches what you must *do,* while the Father teaches us who we can *be*!

When we go back to the parable of the lost son, we see that it is very important to the father that the son returns to the position of sonship. He regards his son, when he was still removed from him and living as an orphan, as . . . dead!

Luke 15:24:

For this son of mine was dead and is alive again; he was lost and is found.' So they began to celebrate.

The cause of *our* problem lies in what we put the focus on. We put sinning (the doing) central and look to God for an answer to our problem. The moment we receive the gift of grace, we are done. But God does not primarily look at what we do, because He puts the focus on who we are. For Him, the most important thing is that we move from being-orphan into sonship. He extends forgiveness to those who still live as an orphan, separated from Him. He does so, not with forgiveness and sin in mind, but for us to receive sonship. Grace and forgiveness are not the goal, but the means by which we reach His goal. It is not primarily about the doing, but about *being!*

Religion teaches what you must do, while the Father teaches us who we can *be*!

The Sandfords

There is a couple who live in the United States who have become very well-known through their ministry and teaching. They have written many books about this. They are John and Paula Sandford. I have mentioned their teaching in Chapter 4. A famous quote of theirs is: *'wounded people, wound people and healed people, heal people.'* They believe that our heart can get wounded and that this affects our life, just like a healed heart affects our life and environment.

During a Father heart conference in England, a close acquaintance of mine posed the following question. She asked: 'Can God's heart also be wounded?' This question intrigued me and I started searching the Bible. I found the following scriptures:

Genesis 6:6:

> The Lord regretted that he had made human beings on the earth, and his heart was deeply **troubled**.

Exodus 3:7:

> The Lord said, 'I have indeed seen the misery of my people in Egypt. I have heard them crying out because of their slave drivers, **and I am concerned about their suffering**.

Here we see a God with pain in His heart. And besides, He has made us in His image and likeness. So, He too knows the emotions and feelings we have. Consider also Christ, how he suffered in the garden of Gethsemane. The answer to the question: can God's heart be wounded? is probably: yes, it can.

And now the second question: if God's heart can be wounded, does the statement of the Sandfords, that a wounded heart wounds others, also apply to God? Whenever I ask this question at a conference, almost everyone agrees that this cannot be the case. The real question, therefore, is, why is it different with the heart of God? And the question following is: does God want it to 'work' differently for us too? Or rather: can our heart be equal in this to His?

(Time to reflect)

> **'If you think you are really preaching grace, yet no one is taking advantage of it, maybe you haven't preached it hard enough or strong enough.' (Charles R. Swindoll – paraphrased)**

The waiting father

Let's take the statement of the Sandfords and take another look at the homecoming of the lost son. What do we see here? We see a son who has made the decision to go home. Probably not driven by a passionate desire to see his father again, but rather because he is hungry and broke. We also see that in spite of his decision return, he is unable to change his identity. He certainly wasn't walking in sonship, he came home as an orphan.

The father sees the son appear in the distance. He has been eagerly waiting, to see if his son would come back. And then the moment arrives, he peers at the road in the distance and recognises the walk of his son. He doesn't think twice and runs towards him! Before his son realises what is happening, the Father takes him in his arms, holds him tightly and passionately kisses him. The son starts his rehearsed story, but doesn't get much further than the first sentence.

In the arms of his father ... he learns that his father still wants to be his father.

And then it happens. Here the transformation takes place. In the arms of his father, in intimacy with him, he learns that his father still wants to be his father. He knows that he can be his son. He experiences closeness, connectedness and intimacy. And this heart-experience transforms the way he thinks. Now he can look his father in the eyes, the shame and disgrace have been taken away. Nothing and nobody can take this away from him. In this moment, the identity of being-orphaned disappears and he receives the identity of sonship.

The wounded father heart

But what happens to the wounded heart of the Father? Why doesn't he first hold his son accountable? How does the father feel about his son's behaviour? These are important questions, because they directly relate to our relationship with God the Father. It is necessary to know the heart of the Father, so that we can receive what He has for us.

So, one more time. The father sees his son appear in the distance. With the joy of his return, the pain also of all the things the son did to him start to surface. The wounds and pain of the past have not disappeared, and the moment of confrontation arises in all its intensity. But how is it possible that the father only responds in love? Here the statement of the Sandfords meets us again. The father experiences the pain of everything the son did to him, but instead of reacting out of this pain, the father realises that wounded people, wound people. It is precisely for this reason that his father heart is moved for his son.

'My son! If you are capable to wound like this what a wounded heart you must have.' The father doesn't react out of the pain he is experiencing, but realises that this wounded, frightful heart only needs healing. He uses his pain as fuel for his love and to bring healing to the heart of his son.

> **The father . . . uses his pain as fuel for his love and to bring healing to the heart of his son.**

With this insight, the image of a God with raised finger (or rod) disappears. God knows that telling an orphan he needs to try harder is of no use, while this is exactly what most of us, most of the time, try to do. But we also know that we can't do it.

His heart rejoices when someone comes to the place where he lets himself be found. The son was at the end of himself, and that was a good thing. When you get to that place, you will stop trying to do it yourself. It brings us to that place where we can surrender our independence and only say: 'Father, here I am.'

The Father is saying to us today, to you: 'Do you believe you're really dependent on Me, and that you are allowed and able to be this? Do you believe that you don't have to first try hard to receive my love? Do you believe that I know your heart is wounded, but that I can heal your heart? Do you believe that I do not primarily look at what you do, but much more at who you are and can be?'

Psalm 84:5 (*The Message*):

> *And how blessed all those in whom you live, whose lives become roads you travel . . .*

Time to reflect:

Try to let this really sink in deeply; what does this mean for you? The verse 'love your enemies' (Matthew 5:44) now appears in a very different light.

To listen:

Brian Doerksen, 'Song for the Prodigals'

Additional reading:

Charles R. Swindoll, *The Grace Awakening* (Nashville, TN: Thomas Nelson, 2012)

Space for notes/reflections:

EIGHT

Peter, James and John

Matthew 4:18-19 (*The Message*):

Walking along the beach of Lake Galilee, Jesus saw two brothers: Simon (later called Peter) and Andrew. They were fishing, throwing their nets into the lake. It was their regular work. Jesus said to them, 'Come with me. I'll make a new kind of fisherman out of you.'

An unexpected turn of events

Jan Kramer of *'Weet-Wie-Je-Bent'* (Know-Who-You-Are) and 'Vaderhart.nl' (previously called 'Epafras Foundation'), organises various conferences every year. One time, he asked me to speak on the apostle Peter at one of these conferences. Seeing as I normally only speak on the Father heart of God, this was a challenge. Would this topic be completely separate from 'my own' topic, or would there be areas that overlapped? I did not expect that it would bring forth such a beautiful revelation before I started. And after the conference this message expanded even more. Thanks, Jan, for setting me on the right course.

Peter, James and John were three of the twelve disciples of Jesus, but not just any three. When you carefully read the relevant passages, you can see that they formed a special group. They had a relationship with Jesus that was different from that of the other disciples. It was a heart relationship that went deeper, and was more intimate.

Let us first take a closer look at Peter. When we do so, we immediately notice certain things. At conferences, I often ask what kind of character Peter is. Before long certain characteristic are called out. He is the 'ringleader', he has a big mouth, but also a small heart. He is robust, unpolished and a real go-getter. He is honest, direct, but also stubborn and impulsive. He is a daredevil and a pioneer, but he also denied Jesus. And Jesus chose him . . .

Matthew 4:18-20:

> As Jesus was walking beside the Sea of Galilee, he saw two brothers, **Simon called Peter** and his brother **Andrew**. They were casting a net into the lake, for they were fishermen. **'Come, follow me,'** Jesus said, 'and **I will send you out to fish for people.'** At once they left their nets and followed him.

The Message:

> They didn't ask questions, but simply **dropped** their nets and followed.

We read in this passage that Jesus asks Peter and his brother Andrew, as the first of the twelve disciples, to follow Him. I believe Andrew was Peter's little brother.

The first disciples

Jesus is on his way to put together a team of people. It is great to see that He doesn't just sit in the temple or the synagogue and sends out a messenger to get Peter and Andrew to meet Him. No, He Himself goes down to meet them where they work and live, where His *'disciples to be'* are living. He goes down to the lake looking for them, and finds them there as fishermen. He even gets *into* their boat to 'learn the ropes'. Here Jesus enters their territory, where they feel at home, and tells them from that old structure about a new way of living.

In the Gospel of Luke, we also see the calling of the first disciples recorded, but here is also mentioned the miraculous catch of fish that happens right before that.

Luke 5:4-7:

> *When he had finished speaking, he said to Simon, 'Put out into deep water, and let down the nets for a catch.' Simon answered, 'Master, we've worked hard all night and haven't caught anything. But because you say so, I will let down the nets.' When they had done so, they caught such a large number of fish that their nets began to break. So they signalled their partners in the other boat to come and help them, and they came and filled both boats so full that they began to sink.*

I have read this passage many times before, but one day, something suddenly jumped out at me that I had never seen before. Of course, it is a true miracle, when after a night of catching nothing, you cast your nets out again at the instructions of Jesus and suddenly you can hardly pull your nets back in due to the amount of fish. Here we see Jesus bringing the supernatural into the natural. But, I thought, isn't it strange when after a whole night of fishing, you haven't even caught one little fish? A small catch I can imagine, but catching absolutely *nothing*? This brings us to the next topic.

The hidden miracle

What makes this miracle even greater, is when we see that another miracle happened right before the miraculous catch of fish. And that is the miraculous catch of *no*-fish! Peter says to Jesus: 'We haven't caught anything!' We can certainly call this a miracle.

What follows, I cannot support biblically, but allow me to take a bit of license when I let my imagination run its course. Could it be (of course, I can't know for sure), that Jesus hid Himself in the bushes on the shore that night and spoke to the fish while the disciples were out on the lake? 'Get away all of you, yes, you, and the little ones too. Everyone go away tonight. You are only to come back in the morning. Take all your friends with you. I will let you know what time you are allowed to come back.'

I think Jesus makes use of two miracles here: 'the miraculous catch of fish' and 'the miraculous catch of no-fish'. It is the stark contrast – having caught nothing, and then having such an enormous amount of fish, even enough to fill up two whole fishing boats – that makes Peter realise here that he is dealing with the supernatural.

Luke 5:8:

> *When Simon Peter saw this, he fell at Jesus' knees and said, 'Go away from me, Lord; I am a sinful man!'*

The Message:

> [Simon Peter:] *'Master, leave. I'm a sinner and can't handle this holiness. Leave me to myself.'*

Jesus then asks Peter to join Him, to follow Him; the decision is quickly made. Without hesitation, they both accept His invitation to follow Him!

Luke 5:9-11:

For he and all his companions were astonished at the catch of fish they had taken, and so were James and John, the sons of Zebedee, Simon's partners. Then Jesus said to Simon, 'Don't be afraid; from now on you will fish for people.' So they pulled their boats up on shore, left everything and followed him.

Fishers of men

Jesus speaks like this: 'from now on you will fish for people', because Peter and Andrew were fishermen. They were still holding their nets! Most of us have kept using this 'quote' of Jesus. Over time, it has been presented to us again and again. But I don't know if it was Jesus' intention for it to be used like this.

Jesus speaks like this: 'from now on you will fish for people', because Peter and Andrew were fishermen.

It was clear that Jesus struck a chord with Peter and Andrew. His words penetrated their hearts. If He had said to them: 'I will make you bakers of living bread', I don't think it would have impacted their hearts as much, and they wouldn't have left their nets behind!

In the same way, God wants to tell you something personally, something that strikes the chord of your heart. It is more than just reading the Word of God. He wants to meet you in the place where you live and He wants to enter your 'old structure', and from that place, introduce you to His new way of living.

It changed their entire lives in an instant! They did not have a prayer meeting to see if this really was from God.

They took the radical step to leave their entire livelihood behind. Wow! God wants to speak to you too in a way you can relate to, that is relevant to you, and touches your heart!

Youth With a Mission

Take Loren Cunningham, for example. He is the founder of Youth With a Mission, a missions organisation that is active all over the world. When he was seventeen years old he lived in Florida, and you could always find him on the beach with a group of friends. Surfing, that was his great passion. That is why God spoke to him in a vision with waves! He saw large waves and these waves changed into many, many young people going out into the world.

> **I think Jesus makes use of two miracles here: 'the miraculous catch of fish' and 'the miraculous catch of no-fish'.**

These examples make less of an impact to someone who has never surfed or been on a fishing boat before. It enters your mind, but it doesn't touch your heart in a way that stirs a passion within you. It is therefore not surprising that we aren't prepared to give up everything right away! In intimacy with the Father, He can speak to you, heart to heart. It is important to have a longing in your heart, to be expectant that He will speak, to stand open, to actively search Him, to direct your gaze towards Him.

Matthew 4:21-22:

Going on from there, he saw two other brothers, **James son of Zebedee and his brother John. They were in a boat with their father Zebedee,** *preparing their nets.*

Jesus called them, and immediately they left the boat and their father and followed him.

Again, we see Jesus calling two brothers to follow Him. Let's try to imagine how this went down.

James:	*'Well, Dad, see you later.'*
Zebedee:	*'What's up, where are you going? The nets aren't ready yet, we will do more fishing later!'*
James:	*'No, we really are leaving now.'*
Zebedee:	*'We? Is John leaving too? Where are you off to?'*
James:	*'Uhm, we don't really know yet.'*
Zebedee:	*'Who are you following, then?'*
James:	*'Well, eh, Him, over there.'*
Zebedee:	*'And can you tell me why you are following Him?'*
James:	*'Well, He called us, and asked us to join Him.'*

Fortunately, we read in the Gospel of Mark that they didn't leave their father completely on his own.

Mark 1:20:

*Without delay he called them, and they left their father Zebedee in the boat with the **hired men** and followed him.*

I can imagine that that evening, at the Zebedee household, the following transpired:

Zebedee:	*'Honey, I'm home!'*
Wife:	*'Great, dinner's ready, are the boys ready too?'*

Zebedee:	*'Eh, no, they're not here . . .'*
Wife:	*'They're still with the boat, are they? Did you catch many fish today?'*
Zebedee:	*'Well, no, and they're not coming home.'*
Wife:	*'What are you saying, Zebbie, what happened?'*
Zebedee:	*'Yep, they left, they joined this Jesus fellow . . .'*

Later on, the mother of James and John enters the story. She probably got to know Jesus a little and it seems like she is now trying to gain some advantage from the situation. She would have said something like this: 'You took my sons away; can we work something out here?'

Matthew 20:20-21:

> *Then the mother of Zebedee's sons came to Jesus with her sons and, kneeling down, asked a favour of him. 'What is it you want?' he asked. She said, 'Grant that one of these two sons of mine may sit at your right and the other at your left in your kingdom.'*

The inner circle

When we read of the disciples, something stands out. It seems like Peter, James and John belonged to a special subgroup. Let's look at a some of these situations. We see that Jesus puts them in a special position within the group of twelve disciples.

Matthew 10:1-4:

> *Jesus called his twelve disciples to him and gave them authority to drive out impure spirits and to heal every*

disease and illness. These are the names of the twelve apostles: **first, Simon (who is called Peter) and his brother Andrew; James son of Zebedee, and his brother John;** *Philip and Bartholomew; Thomas and Matthew the tax collector; James son of Alphaeus, and Thaddaeus; Simon the Zealot and Judas Iscariot, who betrayed him.*

Here Jesus names them from at the top, they are at the start of the list. Andrew is being named at the start as well, as the brother of Peter. But there is more.

Mark 5:35-37:

While Jesus was still speaking, some people came from the house of Jairus, the synagogue leader. 'Your daughter is dead,' they said. 'Why bother the teacher anymore?' Overhearing what they said, Jesus told him, 'Don't be afraid; just believe.' He did not let anyone follow him except **Peter, James and John the brother of James**.

Here Jesus takes Peter, James and John, leaving the others to wait outside. We see that Andrew isn't with them this time. Sometimes Peter's little brother was allowed to join, but he is a bit of a fourth wheel. It's not Peter and Andrew and James and John; but no, Andrew is always named last.

Mark 13:3-4:

As Jesus was sitting on the Mount of Olives opposite the temple, **Peter, James, John and Andrew asked him privately**, *'Tell us, when will these things happen? And what will be the sign that they are all about to be fulfilled?'*

Peter, James and John were probably casually discussing some things. I can imagine that Peter's (little) brother Andrew happened to walk by and asked: 'Can I join you guys?' And he could. When Matthew later records everything, he recalls: 'Oh yes, Andrew was there too', and writes his name down as well; but puts him last.

Relationship and intimacy

The following event tells us something important. We see that Jesus unequivocally corrects Peter, but what kind of effect does this have on their relationship?

Matthew 16:21-23:

> From that time on Jesus began to explain to his disciples that he must go to Jerusalem and suffer many things at the hands of the elders, the chief priests and the teachers of the law, and that he must be killed and on the third day be raised to life. Peter took him aside and began to rebuke him. 'Never, Lord!' he said. 'This shall never happen to you!' **Jesus turned and said to Peter, 'Get behind me, Satan! You are a stumbling-block to me; you do not have in mind the concerns of God, but merely human concerns.'**

Jesus tells His disciples all that is going happen. This is not easy to hear. Up until this point, it's all been too good to be true for them. Jesus is as popular as ever, and they are on His side! And not only that, He involves them, they can 'participate'.

Mark 6:7:

> Calling the Twelve to him, he began to send them out two by two and gave them authority over impure spirits.

The things He tells them now, about suffering and dying, do not sit well. And of course, Peter is the first who thinks he has to address the issue. While Jesus is speaking, Peter signals Him to come over. He says to Jesus: 'Listen here, can we have a chat? I don't want to hear this kind of talk anymore, OK? About all the suffering and such. The people expect something different from us now! We are to stay the course we've been on so far. Do You understand what I'm saying?' How does Jesus respond? He tells Peter what's what, and does it in way so that everyone can hear. For we see Jesus involving the other disciples in this conversation too. He makes them understand very clearly that He determines what direction they will take.

Matthew 16:24:

Then Jesus said to his disciples, 'Whoever wants to be my disciple must deny themselves and take up their cross and follow me.

This is the response of Jesus to the *words* of Peter. But since we can read what happens directly after, we see that the response of Jesus to the person of Peter, is as a friend.

Matthew 17:1:

After six days Jesus took with him Peter, James and John the brother of James, and led them up a high mountain by themselves.

Here we see that *nothing* changed their relationship. Peter hasn't been expelled from the inner circle, their mutual relationship stays the same. What we can deduct from this, is that our relationship and intimacy with Jesus and

> Intimacy ... [is] not a result of our perfection ... but on our answer to the question: 'Do you really love Me?'

God the Father are not a result of our own perfection. We see that our relationship with Him is not dependent on what we do, but on our answer to the question: 'Do you really love Me?' (see John 21:15-17)

In the Gospel of Mark, we read what an amazing experience Peter, James and John had with Jesus. Again, Jesus picks them out of the group of twelve.

Mark 9:2-7:

*After six days Jesus took **Peter, James and John** with him and led them up a high mountain, where they were all alone. There he was transfigured before them. His clothes became dazzling white, whiter than anyone in the world could bleach them. And there appeared before them Elijah and Moses, who were talking with Jesus. Peter said to Jesus, 'Rabbi, it is good for us to be here. Let us put up three shelters – one for you, one for Moses and one for Elijah.' (He did not know what to say, they were so frightened.) Then a cloud appeared and covered them, and a voice came from the cloud: 'This is my Son, whom I love. Listen to him!'*

Not able to follow

When we look at the Gospel of John, we see that 'following', or better yet, the *inability* to follow, is the central theme. It's good for us to realise that the first words Jesus spoke to Peter were: 'Come, follow me' (Matthew 4:19). In the Gospel of John, Jesus says to His disciples: 'I told the Jews that they can't follow Me where I am going, and I am now telling you the same thing.'

This is an important part of the process the disciples are undergoing, but it is also relevant to our own lives. This is the moment in your life when you hit 'the wall'. Peter Scazzero writes about this phenomenon in his book *Emotionally Healthy Spirituality.* Jesus highlights that moment when you cannot rely on your own strength anymore. It's not working anymore, you simply can't go on, no matter how hard you try. It is a wall you can't go around. We can view this as failure, but there is another reason why you encounter the wall. This is the moment when you learn to give up following God in your own strength, and to become totally dependent on Him.

Naturally, it is Peter who responds to this in the manner of: 'I would like to know where exactly You are going. It has to be somewhere pretty extreme if I'm not able to follow You there.'

John 13:31-38:

When he was gone, Jesus said, 'Now the Son of Man is glorified and God is glorified in him. If God is glorified in him, God will glorify the Son in himself, and will glorify him at once. 'My children, I will be with you only a little longer. You will look for me, and just as I told the Jews, so I tell you now: where I am going, you cannot come. A new command I give you: love one another. As I have loved you, so you must love one another. By this everyone will know that you are my disciples, if you love one another.' **Simon Peter asked him, 'Lord, where are you going?' Jesus replied, 'Where I am going, you cannot follow now, but you will follow later.'** *Peter asked, 'Lord, why*

*can't I follow you now? I will lay down my life for you.'
Then Jesus answered, 'Will you really lay down your life
for me? Very truly I tell you, before the cock crows, you
will disown me three times!*

**We see again
that 'wrong
decisions' are
no reason for
Jesus to end the
relationship.**

It doesn't happen very often, but after Jesus addresses Peter again, with everyone there, he is not sure what to say. He is momentarily lost for words when Jesus tells him that he will deny Him three times. Yet, I notice something remarkable here. Jesus announces that Peter is going to deny Him. This is about what Peter *will* do. At the same time, Jesus informs Peter that he will be able to follow Him later. There is no reproach for the denial, no breach of the relationship. Jesus simply looks at the entire situation and opens a new perspective. Amazing!

We see again that 'wrong decisions' are no reason for Jesus to end the relationship. He is indicating here that we are returning from a place of independence to a place where we are totally dependent on the Father. Have things happened in your life, that you believe might influence your relationship with God?

(Time to reflect)

Revelation of a mystery

It seems as if Thomas was out for a while and when he listens to the words of Jesus he suddenly feels as if he has missed something, because how does it work? '"You know the way to the place where I am going'? I have no idea where He is going, how then can we know the way?' I would imagine that the other disciples didn't know either what Jesus meant, but they thought to themselves: I am not going to ask him, before you know you'll be put on the spot like what just happened to Peter. So, they said to Thomas: 'Hey, Thomas, why don't you ask Jesus what He means here?'

John 14:1-7:

> 'Do not let your hearts be troubled. You believe in God; believe also in me. My Father's house has many rooms; if that were not so, would I have told you that I am going there to prepare a place for you? And if I go and prepare a place for you, I will come back and take you to be with me that you also may be where I am. You know the way to the place where I am going.' Thomas said to him, 'Lord, we don't know where you are going, so how can we know the way?' Jesus answered, 'I am the way and the truth and the life. No one comes to the Father except through me. If you really know me, you will know my Father as well. From now on, you do know him and have seen him.'

And now Jesus reveals a mystery to them. He says: 'I am the way and the truth and the life. No one comes to the Father except through me.' It is easy for us to skim over this, because we all know this verse so well. But for the disciples this was revelation. Jesus says here that the Way to the Father is a person, that the Truth is a person and that the Life is a person. He says: 'I am!'

Gethsemane

Matthew 26:36-38:

> Then Jesus went with his disciples to a place called
> Gethsemane, and he said to them, 'Sit here while
> I go over there and pray.' He took **Peter and the two
> sons of Zebedee** along with him, and he began to be
> sorrowful and troubled. Then he said to them, 'My soul
> is overwhelmed with sorrow to the point of death. Stay
> here and keep watch with me.'

At this moment, apart from Judas, all the disciples were with
Jesus in the garden of Gethsemane. Again, He takes only
Peter, James and John, leaving the others. Jesus shares His
heart with them. He tells them He is *terrified*! He shares
His heart with an unrestrained intensity. I will return to this
later in the book. This stands in stark contrast to the fact that
Peter will shortly deny Him three times.

John 18:25-27:

> Meanwhile, **Simon Peter** was still standing there warming
> himself. So they asked him, 'You aren't one of his disciples
> too, are you?' He denied it, saying, 'I am not.' One of the
> high priest's servants, a relative of the man whose ear
> Peter had cut off, challenged him, 'Didn't I see you with
> him in the garden?' **Again Peter denied it, and at that
> moment a cock began to crow.**

Jesus is taken away and later crucified. After His death, the
disciples must have been in shock for some time. We know
the whole story, that Jesus was crucified, died and rose again.
But at this moment in time, what overshadowed their lives
was that they lost Him. He had died! And that was a fact.

And Peter had to live with the fact that he didn't have the courage to say that he belonged to Him. Jesus was right, *he* was unable to follow Him.

Some of the disciples were now together and had no idea how to carry on. For three years, they had followed Jesus. What now? Sometime after they were walking the shores of the lake, probably even the same spot where Peter had left his nets to follow Jesus. In any case, Peter returns three years later and says to the others: 'You know what? I'm going fishing.'

John 21:2-3:

> *Simon Peter, Thomas (also known as Didymus), Nathanael from Cana in Galilee, the sons of Zebedee, and two other disciples were together.* **'I'm going out to fish,' Simon Peter told them**, *and they said, 'We'll go with you.' So they went out and got into the boat, but that night they caught nothing.*

Can you imagine? Peter, totally frustrated by everything that has happened. He who is usually the first and wants to show others that he can take care of things. He walked on water, he defended Jesus at the garden with his sword. And now he has failed terribly. He has lost all perspective; he is likely at the end of his rope. The only thing he can think of right now is to fall back on what he knows best: fishing! And that is what he decides to do, and six others decide join him.

The miraculous catch of no-fish, the repeat

But this time they can't even do what they normally do best. They were out on the lake all night and caught nothing! Now Peter is really at the end of himself. He has come to the place where he can do nothing of himself. And then, precisely at *that* moment, there He is . . .

John 21:4-6:

> *Early in the morning, Jesus stood on the shore, but the disciples did not realise that it was Jesus. He called out to them, 'Friends, haven't you any fish?' 'No,' they answered. He said, 'Throw your net on the right side of the boat and you will find some.' When they did, they were unable to haul the net in because of the large number of fish.*

Jesus calls out from the shore: 'Hello, have you got any fish on board?' Of course, He knows that is not the case. The disciples are so frustrated from the night, that their only reply is a short 'no'. But Jesus has different intentions with this question. He is about to do the exact same thing He did when He asked them to follow Him the first time.

A lot has happened since then. It all started with that first invitation: 'Come, follow me' (Matthew 4:19). But later on, Jesus also said: 'Where I am going, you cannot follow now' (John 13:36). After a three-year *internship* – in which they have climbed the highest mountaintops with Jesus, but also went through the deepest valleys – they are about to enter a completely new phase.

> **The highest lesson they have learned, is that they cannot follow Jesus in their own strength.**

The highest lesson they have learned is that they cannot follow Jesus in their own strength. They had to personally experience this. It might feel like failing, but Jesus has a different perspective. Basically,

He is saying that this is the most important lesson you can learn, bringing you out of independence and your own strength into a relationship of dependence.

Jesus wants to let them know that all is well, the plan hasn't been changed: it continues. They are moving into a new phase. It is wonderful to see that Jesus communicates this by doing the exact same miracle as when He first asked them to follow Him. Better yet, we see here both the miraculous catch of fish, as well as the miraculous catch of *no*-fish!

A déjà vu and a new start

The moment Jesus tells them to cast out their nets again, a light begins to dawn on Peter. They went through this before. This is how it all started! Where first, Peter was completely at the end of himself and unable follow, there is now new hope and expectation filling his heart. 'Yes, I will definitely cast out my net on the other side, I know what's going to happen!'

When the disciples decided to go fishing, they went back to square one, back to their 'old' lives. But Jesus is showing them that there is a continuation, that the time of 'not being able to follow' is over. It is wonderful that Jesus communicates this by coming to them. And, it is also wonderful to see that He shows by a new miraculous catch of fish that the relationship is still intact, but there is a new beginning, a new invitation to follow Him.

The disciples come to a place within themselves where they wanted to return to their old, plain lives. From Jesus' point of view, however, they had come to a point in their lives where moving forward in their own strength was no longer an option; they were ready to come into total dependency. And that is not something you can *learn*, you have to *experience* it.

Spiritual and natural living?

The disciples made a distinction. The 'spiritual' journey with Jesus had clearly come to an end. Therefore, being professional fishermen, they returned to the 'natural'. But even in doing so they failed. There was simply nothing left for them. Then Jesus shows up. He doesn't make the distinction between whether you are occupied with 'spiritual' matters or everyday ordinary things. He shows that in that place of total dependency, He has the answer. He simply wants to show you that He can – and wants to – be involved in every aspect of your life.

John 21:7-9:

> *Then the disciple whom Jesus loved said to Peter, 'It is the Lord!' As soon as Simon Peter heard him say, 'It is the Lord,' he wrapped his outer garment round him (for he had taken it off) and jumped into the water. The other disciples followed in the boat, towing the net full of fish, for they were not far from shore, about a hundred metres. When they landed, they saw a fire of burning coals there with fish on it, and some bread.*

Naturally, it is Peter who cannot wait and jumps overboard. Is it really Jesus? How is that possible? is it really Him? But Peter still has some mixed feelings. He certainly hasn't forgotten the fact that he denied Him three times. But what about Jesus? He doesn't mention anything. He only says: 'Come, let us first get together and eat.'

John 21:10-14:

> *Jesus said to them, 'Bring some of the fish you have just caught.' So Simon Peter climbed back into the boat and dragged the net ashore. It was full of large fish, 153, but even with so many the net was not torn. Jesus said to them, 'Come and have breakfast.' None of the disciples dared ask him, 'Who are you?' They knew it was the Lord. Jesus came, took the bread and gave it to them, and did the same with the fish. This was now the third time Jesus appeared to his disciples after he was raised from the dead.*

Then, after the meal, Jesus raises the issue of Peter's denial of Him. But Jesus doesn't stand in judgement, or even resentment. He responds to Peter's denial with love and restoration. He speaks privately to him: '[Peter], do you love me more than these?' What we cannot directly see in the translated text that here Jesus uses the word *agape*. He says to Peter; do you love Me unconditionally? Of course, Peter would rather have said: 'Yes Lord, I love you unconditionally.' But he was well aware that when it mattered most, he did in fact deny Him. He couldn't therefore say that he loved Jesus unconditionally. So, he took it down a notch, and said: 'Yes, Lord ... you know that I love you.' Here Peter doesn't use the word *agape*, but the word *phileo*, which is the brotherly kind of love, which stands for friendship. The second time, Jesus asks Peter the question if he loves Him; again He uses the word *agape*. And Peter again responds with *phileo*. When Jesus asks him the same question a third time, He meets him half way and also uses the word *phileo*.

[Jesus] responds to Peter's denial with love and restoration.

John 21:15-17:

> When they had finished eating, Jesus said to **Simon Peter, 'Simon son of John,** do you love **[agape]** me more than these?' 'Yes, Lord,' he said, 'you know that I love **[phileo]** you.' Jesus said, 'Feed my lambs.' Again Jesus said, 'Simon son of John, do you love **[agape]** me?' He answered, 'Yes, Lord, you know that I love **[phileo]** you.' Jesus said, 'Take care of my sheep.' The third time he said to him, 'Simon son of John, do you love me?' Peter was hurt because Jesus asked him the third time, 'Do you love **[phileo]** me?' He said, 'Lord, you know all things; you know that I love **[phileo]** you.' Jesus said, 'Feed my sheep.

Out of this love, out of this friendship, Jesus instructs Peter to care for His lambs and sheep. This is a very different thing than to work for God and be rewarded for it!

You might be thinking, *phileo* love is less than *agape* love, but that indeed is the question. That time when Jesus declared that He is totally dependent on the Father, it states in the following verse: 'For the Father loves the Son'. Whenever I ask at a conference which of the loves is mentioned here, almost everyone assumes it is *agape* love. Yet the word that is used here is *phileo*, the friendship or brotherly love, not the unconditional *agape* love.

John 5:19-20:

> Jesus gave them this answer: 'Very truly I tell you, the Son can do nothing by himself; he can do only what he sees his Father doing, because whatever the Father does the Son also does. For the Father loves the Son and shows him all he does. Yes, and he will show him even greater works than these, so that you will be amazed.

There is a simple explanation. God the Father first loves with *agape* love, because He wants to get His children back.

John 3:16:

> For God so loved [agape] the world that he gave his one and only Son, that whoever believes in him shall not perish but have eternal life.

At this point we haven't done anything to deserve the love of the Father. That is why it's necessary that He begins with unconditional love. But in the intended relationship He has with His children, there is more beyond the unconditional love, the love that doesn't expect anything in return. That is why the Father mentions *phileo* love to Jesus. The Father enjoys it when He can expect love in return from His Son.

This is where Jesus finally finishes with Peter. A double lesson. Firstly, Jesus taught Peter that no matter how much effort you put into it, you cannot generate *agape* love within yourself. Secondly, Jesus indicates that for Him, it is all about a mutual relationship. This has in the first place nothing to do with actions, and everything to do with the state of the heart.

The restored relationship

In this beautiful episode, we see both a broken, and a restored Peter. His independency was broken, then, in dependency, Peter was accepted and restored. The commission from Jesus to Peter came out of a response of the love Peter showed and

His independency was broken, then, in dependency, Peter was accepted and restored.

expressed to Jesus. Trust also springs forth out of this love and it becomes easy to trust Him in matters. Trust and love, out of friendship.

John 21:18-22:

> *Very truly I tell you, when you were younger you dressed yourself and went where you wanted; but when you are old you will stretch out your hands, and someone else will dress you and lead you where you do not want to go.' Jesus said this to indicate the kind of death by which Peter would glorify God. Then he said to him,* **'Follow me!'** *Peter turned and saw that the disciple whom Jesus loved was following them. (This was the one who had leaned back against Jesus at the supper and had said, 'Lord, who is going to betray you?') When Peter saw him, he asked, 'Lord, what about him?' Jesus answered, 'If I want him to remain alive until I return, what is that to you?* **You must follow me.'**

How very intimate, that Jesus' final words to Peter are the exact same words that He started with on the journey with him: 'Follow Me.' Jesus began with the challenge to follow Him. You can, using your own free will, which is given to every human being, make a decision to follow Him.

Matthew 4:19 (NKJV):

> *Then He said to them, 'Follow Me, and I will make you fishers of men.'*

Then comes the moment when He reveals to you that you cannot continue in your own strength, but that it is important to come into a relationship of dependency.

John 13:36:

> *Simon Peter asked him, 'Lord, where are you going?'*
> *Jesus replied, 'Where I am going, you cannot follow now,*
> *but you will follow later.'*

Personal

Maybe you've experienced something like this in a similar way. The time of 'not being able to follow' is there for a reason. Strangely enough, the 'inability to follow' brought Peter to a place he would not have been able to reach by himself. It brought him to the place of being dependent. It is thus important when you experience difficult times, to ask the Father to reveal to you what is going on. Are the difficulties brought about by the enemy, and do you need to pray against it, and pray that the difficulties must leave in Jesus' Name? Or could it be that God wants to bring you to a place of *brokenness*, where you realise that you cannot do 'it' by yourself, so that He can bring you to a place of total dependency on Him, and afterwards will say to you, having arrived at the new place:

John 21:19:

> *Then he said to him,* **'Follow me!'**

Different groups of disciples

The chapter seems to end here, and it is a great ending, but one question still remains. Why was there the group of three within the group of twelve disciples? Does Jesus have favourites, or is that a strange question? Does Jesus have to like you enough for you to be part of that intimate little group, perhaps when you (almost) never make a mistake?

That is obviously not the case, because Peter didn't measure up to this standard either. I think this has to be approached from a different perspective. Jesus does not have favourites, but He wants to show us that *we* may, and can choose. So there are in fact different groups of people.

Firstly, there is the *multitude*. They come to listen to Jesus and perhaps you can compare them to the people who 'just' go to church once a week. Does Jesus love these people? Of course He loves them.

Then there are the *seventy-two* (see Luke 10). They were involved, were sent out, were given an assignment. Does Jesus love these seventy-two? Of course He loves them.

Then there are the *twelve disciples*. They were the ones who spent three entire years with Jesus. For three full years they experienced everything with Him. Does Jesus love 'His twelve'? Of course, with all His heart.

Now we have the *group of three*. They have shared the most intimate moments with Jesus. This relationship between Jesus and Peter, James and John was deep!

And finally, there is *us*: how do we relate to Jesus – which group do we belong to? Jesus says: 'You get to choose. The question is, which group do you *want* to belong to?' Coming back to dependency is the key to having a relationship with God the Father. This puts the challenge before us, before you. Intimacy is not the result of perfection, but the answer we give to the question: 'Do you really love Me?'

Time to reflect:

Try to let this really sink in. What does it mean for you? When you choose to belong to the group of three, what ramifications does that have on your life (with God)? Make it tangible, make a list, write something down!

To listen:

CD: Brian & Jenn Johnson, *'Where You Go I Go'*

Additional reading:

Peter Scazzero, *Emotionally Healthy Spirituality (Grand Rapids, MI: Zondervan, 2017)*

Websites:

Jan Kramer, *'Weet-Wie-Je-Bent'* (Know-Who-You-Are) and www.vaderhart.nl

Loren Cunningham, Youth with a Mission, www.ywam.org and www.ywam.nl

Space for notes/reflections:

NINE

Do not be afraid

Matthew 11:27-28 (*The Message*):

This is a unique Father-Son operation, coming out of Father and Son intimacies and knowledge. No one knows the Son the way the Father does, nor the Father the way the Son does. . . . Are you tired? Worn out? Burned out on religion? Come to me. Get away with me and you'll recover your life. I'll show you how to take a real rest. Walk with me and work with me – watch how I do it. Learn the unforced rhythms of grace. I won't lay anything heavy or ill-fitting on you. Keep company with me and you'll learn to live freely and lightly.

Our image of the Father

In the chapter about the parable of the five wise and foolish virgins, I already mentioned the fear Adam and Eve had of God after the Fall. However, it is important to make a distinction between having a 'fear' of God, that is, fearing Him or being afraid of Him, and the 'fear of the Lord', which means that you honour and reverence Him. God the Father **never** meant for us to fear Him. Fear is the opposite of love and intimacy. Fear is there to evade danger, but it is also used for control and manipulation or to dominate others. Love, on the other hand, will always respect your God-given, free will.

We previously established that before the Fall, Adam and Eve were not afraid of God. We concluded that sin changes our image of Him. A wrong image of God greatly influences the way we live our lives. We have been created to live and function in total unity with God the Father. The Bible tells us that we have been created in His image and likeness. So, when we have a wrong image of the Father who created us, we can see the effects of this in who we are. The image we have of God determines what He can do through us! Sin changes our image of God.

(Time to reflect)

Trusting God completely

One of the songs of Hillsong United, 'Oceans (Where Feet May Fail)', contains lyrics about being led where we need to trust in God completely. These words really speak to me. Knowing it's possible, our image of the Father being so completely restored, that we feel completely safe in the intimacy of His presence, and that we can personally trust Him for everything! Wow!

How do we get to that place? Are there blockages? It seems almost too obvious that to find the answer, we have to return again to the place where it all began, the garden of Eden. I believe that *before* the Fall, Adam and Eve knew no fear or shame. It says:

Genesis 2:25:

> Adam and his wife were both **naked, and they felt no shame.**

This, however, changed after the Fall. We see sin having an effect on their relationship with God, as well as on their relationship with each other. They changed and they now fear the Other, who hasn't changed.

Genesis 3:9-10:

> But the Lord God called to the man, 'Where are you?' He answered, 'I heard you in the garden, and **I was afraid** because I was **naked**; so I hid.'

When you have a wrong image of God, and you believe, for example, that He is angry with you, you can easily interpret the words 'Where are you?' as: 'Oh no, He is coming, He found out . . . quickly, get away!' But hiding from God is not going to work, so you have to face the confrontation. And with trembling legs, Adam starts his defence.

We have previously established that next to hearing God's voice, it is even more important to know the One who is speaking. Your image of God will always influence the spoken word of God. You interpret that what you hear through the image you have of Him. So, the question is: can we discover a God of love in that moment when He kicks His children out of the garden?

Genesis 3:23:

> So the Lord God banished him from the Garden of Eden to work the ground from which he had been taken.

Perhaps you have also thought that it makes sense for God to punish them for what they did and banish them from the garden. But what do you make of what happens next? God the Father created Adam and Eve as His children, the crown of His creation. What God loves most is *being* Father. It is His desire to love many children, and to enjoy them while

The Father who now enters the garden and says: 'Where are you?' is a Father with tears in His eyes and a broken heart. He has just 'lost' His children.

He leads them into the fulfilment of their destiny. He has been able to enjoy His two children, Adam and Eve, for some time. But now the relationship is prematurely and abruptly broken. The Father who now enters the garden and says: 'Where are you?' is a Father with tears in His eyes and a broken heart. He has just 'lost' His children.

He knows there is another tree in the middle of the garden, the Tree of Life. Because of this tree, He leads them out of the garden, so that they can't eat from it. Why? Because if they did, they would forever be separated from the Father. However, the Father has already a rescue and restoration plan ready. Until this plan is completed, access to the Tree of Life is forbidden.

Genesis 3:24:

> *After he drove the man out, he placed on the east side of the Garden of Eden cherubim and a flaming sword flashing back and forth to guard the way to the tree of life.*

Looking at the situation from this perspective, we get a very different image of God than the image of an angry Father.

Do not be afraid – come to Me

What a wonderful invitation! Here God completely reveals Himself as a loving Father who loves His children very much, and . . . you may come as you are. Still, we see that through sin, fear entered the human race. We can find many examples of this in the Old Testament, but we would also like to find a solution: how can we find the place where we can be in His presence without fear?

Zechariah

We start the New Testament with Zechariah. He was the priest chosen by lot to go into the temple and be of service at the altar of incense. Now the time comes to go into the altar of incense, and he is pretty nervous. 'Have I done everything right, is it good enough for God?' He moves from the outer courts past the first veil and enters the Holy of Holies and . . . nothing happens. 'So far so good,' he thinks to himself. And then, suddenly, the angel Gabriel appears right next to him, surrounded by the glory of God. 'Aaaahhhhhhh!' In his mind, Zechariah already sees the angel draw his sword. Surely, he has come to kill him! Zechariah's eyes are filled with fear.

By the way, Zechariah didn't think: 'Oh, Gabriel, how nice! Do you come here often, or only on special occasions? I'm a big fan of yours, meeting you was at the top of my bucket list.' He also didn't say: 'Hey, Gabriel, I hope you don't mind, but can I touch your wings?' Nothing of the sort. Zechariah was simply terrified.

Luke 1:11-13:

Then an angel of the Lord appeared to him, standing at the right side of the altar of incense. When Zechariah saw him, he was startled and was gripped with fear. But the angel said to him: 'Do not be afraid, Zechariah; your prayer has been heard. Your wife Elizabeth will bear you a son, and you are to call him John.

It's good to see what happens here. The angel delivers a glorious message, for he tells Zechariah that the long-cherished dream of his wife, Elizabeth, will come true. They had prayed so long for a baby, and now an angel, the angel Gabriel, comes to bring them this wonderful news!

However, the priest who was chosen to bring the offer of incense before the Lord is in fear the moment the glory of God appears. It is important to realise here that it is not talking about fear as 'the fear of the Lord'. It is not talking about a reverence of God, for then the angel Gabriel wouldn't have told Zechariah not to be afraid. Just like Adam, Zechariah was also afraid when the glory of God appeared. Fear is one of the biggest hindrances of coming into intimacy, while God wants to use His glory to make us one with Him. It is even our destiny to carry his glory, so that the world would see who God really is: a loving Father!

Fear is one of the biggest hindrances of coming into intimacy ...

John 17:22-23:

> I have given them the glory that you gave me, **that they may be one as we are one** – I in them and you in me – so that they may be brought to complete unity. **Then the world will know** that you sent me and have loved them even as you have loved me.

Visiting Mary

A little while later, the angel Gabriel makes another visit; this time he came to Mary. I imagine that Mary was going about her daily chores in her little home. There were no dishwashers in those days, so she might well have been busy with the dishes when the angel suddenly entered her house. When the angel Gabriel appears in all his glory, we see here too that Mary is afraid!

Luke 1:30:

> But the angel said to her, '**Do not be afraid**, Mary, you have found favour with God.

This is a good place to pause and remember the time before the Fall. God the Father came into the garden daily, in all His glory, and nowhere before the Fall do we read that He told Adam not to be afraid. Through sin, our image of God was changed. But today God is taking counter measures. He came with the revelation of the Father heart and the time is coming that we will not only have no fear when His glory appears, but that we ourselves will be carriers of His glory.

The shepherds

Again, the angel appears, and this time he is visiting the shepherds in the field.

Luke 2:8-10:

> And there were shepherds living out in the fields near by, keeping watch over their flocks at night. An angel of the Lord appeared to them, and the glory of the Lord shone around them, **and they were terrified**. But the angel said to them, '**Do not be afraid**. I bring you good news that will cause great joy for all the people.

Here we read that the shepherds were not just afraid, they were 'terrified'! Why? I think they became aware of all the mistakes they had made in their lives and they feared, at the revealing of so many angels, the consequence, the punishment of God.

The disciples

But it was not only the shepherds who were afraid. We see the same happening to the disciples when they were in the boat on the lake.

Matthew 14:26-33:

> When the disciples saw him walking on the lake, they were terrified. 'It's a ghost,' they said, and cried out in fear. But Jesus immediately said to them: 'Take courage! **It is I. Don't be afraid.'** 'Lord, if it's you,' Peter replied, 'tell me to come to you on the water.' 'Come,' he said. Then Peter got down out of the boat, walked on the water and came towards Jesus. **But when he saw the wind, he was afraid and, beginning to sink, cried out, 'Lord, save me!'** Immediately Jesus reached out his hand and caught him. 'You of little faith,' he said, 'why did you **doubt**?' And when they climbed into the boat, the wind died down. Then those who were in the boat worshipped him, saying, 'Truly you are the Son of God.'

Every time we hear the same thing: 'Don't be afraid.' It looks like God wants to communicate something to us. Through the revelation of the heart of the Father we discover God being our personal Father who wants to care for us, who wants to protect us. He says: 'I am your Father, you don't have to fear Me. I want to fill you with My love.' What He is saying with 'it is I' is that we can know Him for who He really is, the answer to all fear.

Psalm 23:4:

> Even though I walk through the darkest valley, **I will fear no evil, for you are with me**; your rod and your staff, they comfort me.

John at Patmos

The observing reader will recognise that these examples involve people who had not yet experienced a *spiritual* birth (being born again). Neither Zechariah nor Mary, nor the shepherds or the disciples, none of them were born again. That's why we now will go to John's book of Revelation, where we read:

Revelation 1:17-18

> When I saw him, I fell at his feet as though dead. Then he placed his right hand on me and said: '**Do not be afraid**. I am the First and the Last. I am the Living One; I was dead, and now look, I am alive for ever and ever! And **I hold the keys of death and Hades.**

Here we don't just read of anyone. This is John, the apostle whom Jesus loved. He was part of the inner circle of three disciples (Peter, James and John) who Jesus shared His heart with. And here it says that when he saw Jesus, he feared for his life. How is that possible? For John, this had to be more than just an encounter with the Jesus he spent three years of his life with. Here, John stood face-to-face with Jesus in all His glory, and we see what kind of effect it had on John. This account therefore shows that being born again alone does not automatically restore intimacy.

Where do we find the answer, then?

It is, in fact, John who gives us the answer. He writes about it in his first letter.

1 John 4:18:

> There is no fear in love. But perfect love drives out fear, because **fear has to do with punishment**. The one who fears is not made perfect in love.

John says here that when we are one with God the Father, He can fill us with His love, because God is love (1 John 4:8). The great thing is that we don't have to try to drive out fear, this is God's work in us. He reveals to us again that through dependency on Him, He will care for us. As long as we keep preaching the punishment and law of God, as long as this mindset is in our system, we will not discover true intimacy with God the Father, and we will only relate to Him from afar. It is tremendously important to recognise this reality.

The only person I know of who saw the glory of God and was not afraid, is Stephen.

But at that moment he was facing death.

Acts 7:55-56:

> But Stephen, full of the Holy Spirit, looked up to heaven and **saw the glory of God, and Jesus** standing at the right hand of God. 'Look,' he said, 'I see heaven open and the Son of Man standing at the right hand of God.'

How do we enter into intimacy with God?

Sometimes I hear people say it is good to have a reverence for God and stay at an appropriate distance of Him, because He is the Almighty. Having honour and reverence for God is certainly not wrong. I do think we have to ask ourselves the question, though, if it is hindering intimacy between God the Father and us. It's helpful to consider what a good father would do.

I believe in this time that the revelation of the Father heart of God can bring the Church to a place where she's never been before. The Church, as the bride of Christ, is by definition meant to come into intimacy.

The Father always meant for us to come into intimacy with Him, that we would really come know Him as Father, that we would receive His love and live in the intimacy of sonship and receive healing in our hearts. He is always calling: 'Do not be afraid...come to Me!' Through intimacy, you receive your identity and this is how you can reach your destiny.

When, though intimacy, we gain a limitless trust, when we, through this trust, are able to be dependent, when, in this place of dependency, we are filled with love, when, though total love, fear disappears, *then* we are able to carry the splendour, the glory of God and *then* the world will see who God is!

Through intimacy, you receive your identity and this is how you can reach your destiny.

Time to reflect:

When you realise that you don't yet know the Father in intimacy, do not be afraid. He longs for this relationship more than you. Talk to Him, tell Him that you want to know Him better. Take the time to experience His presence.

To listen:

Bethel Music, 'No Longer Slaves'

And

Hillsong United, 'Oceans (Where Feet May Fail)'

Additional reading:

Floyd McClung, *The Father Heart of God* (Eastbourne: Kingsway, 2007)

Websites:

Johannes Hartl, https://johanneshartl.org and https://gebethaus.org

Space for notes/reflections:

TEN

Two women

2 Corinthians 3:3 (*The Message*):

Your very lives are a letter that anyone can read by just looking at you. Christ himself wrote it – not with ink, but with God's living Spirit; not chiseled into stone, but carved into human lives – and we publish it.

The bleeding woman

This chapter I would like to talk about the similarities and differences between the Bible as the Word of God, and Jesus the Son of God as the Living Word.

The account of the bleeding woman is recorded in several Gospels. For twelve years, she suffered this disease and had tried absolutely everything to obtain her healing. She had spent all of her money, but nothing had worked. Her condition had even grown worse.

Mark 5:25-26:

And a woman was there who had been subject to bleeding for twelve years. She had suffered a great deal under the care of many doctors and had spent all she had, yet instead of getting better she grew worse.

Twelve years? That is a long time! What did this woman suffer all these years? Besides suffering the disease, there was also the grief of being rejected by the entire community. What does the law state (the Word of God)?

Leviticus 15:19-20:

> When a woman has her regular flow of blood, the impurity of her monthly period will last seven days, and anyone who touches her will be unclean till evening. Anything she lies on during her period will be unclean, and anything she sits on will be unclean.

This topic continues until verse 25, summarising situations in which the impurity of a woman makes others unclean. In verse 25 is also mentioned that the same applies to a woman bleeding outside her monthly period of uncleanness.

Leviticus 15:24-25:

> If a man has sexual relations with her and her monthly flow touches him, he will be unclean for seven days; any bed he lies on will be unclean. When a woman has a discharge of blood for many days at a time other than her monthly period or has a discharge that continues beyond her period, she will be unclean as long as she has the discharge, just as in the days of her period.

The flow of blood was of enormous consequence to this woman. Imagine, you're sick, you've been sick for a very long time, but there is no one to put a comforting arm around you. There is no one who will sit beside you to hold your hand and show compassion. Because of this disease and what the law states, social contact was simply impossible. If someone came into contact with her, they would be unclean as well, just like this woman. She was very much living as an outcast. In India, there are those who are called Dalits, the untouchables. This woman was like one of them.

For twelve years, she was unclean. This means for twelve years no access to the synagogue, for twelve years no temple access. She was cut off from all social contacts and so even her spiritual life had come under pressure. For twelve years, no intimacy . . . The effect of the disease on the life of this woman was more than just a physical problem. This woman must have known a deep emotional pain as well.

This woman had a calling on her life, just like any other person, but she was unable to fulfil it. As a human being she was designed to have *fellowship*. She was created by a God of love to love and to be loved. Yet she was in a position where this was out of her reach. For twelve years, life was flowing out of her. In her quest for healing and restoration her situation had only become worse. You'd think this woman would have given up all hope.

New hope

When I read this story again, it occurred to me that even after twelve years, this woman had not given up. When she heard the stories of Jesus, new hope arose in her.

Mark 5:27-28:

> When she heard about Jesus, she came up behind him in the crowd and touched his cloak, because she thought, 'If I just touch his clothes, I will be healed.'

I think even despite her troubles she had not lost her faith. We don't read anything about that, but it wouldn't surprise me if she had received a revelation of God the Father. It is not the kind of idea you come up with by yourself: to worm your way through a large crowd as an unclean woman, only to then touch a rabbi and believe this will heal you . . .

This account may have something to do with what Jesus later refers to as 'greater works'. Most of us know this verse, but not many know what He exactly meant by it. How can you do greater works than Jesus?

John 14:12 (NKJV):

Most assuredly, I say to you, he who believes in Me, the works that I do he will do also; and greater works than these he will do, because I go to My Father.

How can you do greater works than Jesus?

Whenever, during a conference, I ask people to name some examples of these 'greater works', they will often answer with 'the greater numbers of converts' we see in recent history due to the increase of global access. But I have not yet come across anyone who has been able to give me a satisfying answer. At some point though, I realised that John 14 was not the first time that 'greater works' were mentioned. To my surprise, these greater works were first assigned to Jesus.

John 5:19-20:

Jesus gave them this answer: 'Very truly I tell you, the Son can do nothing by himself; he can do only what he sees his Father doing, because whatever the Father does the Son also does. For the Father loves the Son and shows him all he does. Yes, and he will show him even greater works than these, so that you will be amazed.

This comes right after the verse where Jesus says He can do nothing of Himself. Interesting in that here He says *the Father* will show Him 'greater works'! The same is true for us. Here it is not about us. It is all about the Father. He is central. The only thing asked of us is that we don't put limitations on Him. Of us it is asked that we not only believe what we have seen Him do before, but believe He can also do things He has never done before ... through us!

Back to the woman

This is precisely what the woman in this story does. No one was ever healed of a flow of blood in this way; by touching the hem of the garment of a rabbi. It even seems to contradict the law, but we will return to this later.

What was going on inside this woman when this idea came to her? It must have been a combination of hope, faith but also anxiety and fear. Maybe there were a number of times when she nearly decided not to do it. But finally, her faith won. Most likely she would have covered herself completely, in something like a burqa, perhaps. For she had to move through the crowd of people and after twelve years, everyone knew that she was the unclean woman. But she was ready and prepared, and waited for Jesus to pass by. When she saw Him, she pushed through the crowd, until she was close enough behind Him that she could touch his garment.

Mark 5:29:

Immediately her bleeding stopped and she felt in her body that she was freed from her suffering.

Immediately . . .

What a moment that must have been! She immediately noticed that she was better. After twelve long years, finally healed! What joy, it was almost incomprehensible what just happened here. But then something else happens. Jesus stops and looks around. He says: 'Who touched Me?' She holds her breath and probably wonders what she's done now. She, an unclean woman, touching a rabbi! What will He say, how will He react?

Mark 5:30-34:

At once Jesus realised that power had gone out from him. He turned round in the crowd and asked, 'Who touched my clothes?' 'You see the people crowding against you,' his disciples answered, 'and yet you can ask, 'Who touched me?' But Jesus kept looking around to see who had done it. Then the woman, knowing what had happened to her, came and fell at his feet and, trembling with fear, told him the whole truth. He said to her, 'Daughter, your faith has healed you. Go in peace and be freed from your suffering.'

Then Jesus looks at her and she looks into His loving eyes and there she meets the Father who lives in Him.

Why does Jesus want to 'expose' this woman? Everything had gone smoothly for her, no one had recognised her, and she was healed after all. Yet, Jesus says: 'Who touched Me?' He looks around and at that moment the woman makes herself known to Him. But not only to Jesus, she exposes herself to the entire surrounding crowd of people. She tells Him everything that happened. Then Jesus looks at her and she looks into His loving eyes and there she meets the Father who lives in Him. This moment instantaneously heals twelve years of emotional pain and frustration. Now she is not only physically, but also within herself, a healed woman.

After Jesus had spoken to her, she gets up and the people move aside to let her through, but this time not because of her uncleanness, but out of reverence. With head held high, she walks back to her house, healed and clean.

Jesus and the law

We will need return to Leviticus 15 for a moment. For here it says: '. . . and anyone who touches her will be unclean till evening' (verse 19). According to the law, Jesus should be unclean after this woman had touched Him. Did this happen, though? The answer is, of course, that He did not become unclean. So, what then is going on here?

The Word of God comes from God, and in the Word of God, the law was given by God. The law, however, is given to the sinner, so that he can recognise what sin is. Jesus *is* the Living Word of God.

John 1:1,14:

> *In the beginning was the Word, and the Word was with God, and the Word was God . . .*
> *The Word became flesh and made his dwelling among us. We have seen his glory, the glory of the one and only Son, who came from the Father, full of grace and truth.*

Because Jesus never knew sin, the law does not apply to Him. He is not under the law. For this reason, He does not become unclean by the touch of the unclean woman. On the contrary, the power of the life that Jesus carries within Himself is so strong that disease and uncleanness have to give way and the woman becomes clean when she touches Him.

In Luke 16, Jesus refers to the law. Here He says two things that seem to contradict each other.

Luke 16:16-17:

The Law and the Prophets were proclaimed until John. Since that time, the good news of the kingdom of God is being preached, and everyone is forcing their way into it. It is easier for heaven and earth to disappear than for the least stroke of a pen to drop out of the Law.

On the one hand, He says that the 'Law and the Prophets were . . . until John', this is the dividing line. On the other hand, though, He says that the law will not disappear. What He means here, is that everything the prophets have spoken about has become reality, and He came to fulfil the law. This does not dismiss or abolish the law. However, through Jesus it has become possible for us to come out from under the law. By this the law has no power to judge us any longer. It his letter to the Galatians, Paul makes this very clear, for it says:

Galatians 5:18:

But if you are led by the Spirit, you are not under the law.

When we really grasp this, it will literally change our position in the world!

(Time to reflect)

The law of Moses, grace and truth

This story most likely happened in Capernaum, in Israel. Israel is the holy land, with the holy city and the holy temple and the holy Word of God. This is the land of the people of the holy God, the God of heaven and earth. And they had received this Word of God, as the law of Moses.

Deuteronomy 10:10-11:

Now I had stayed on the mountain forty days and forty nights, as I did the first time, and the Lord listened to me at this time also. It was not his will to destroy you. 'Go,' the Lord said to me, 'and lead the people on their way, so that they may enter and possess the land I swore to their ancestors to give them.'

So, there are the Pharisees and teachers of the law. Even though they were greatly occupied with the Word, it appears they had found no solution for this woman. Despite living in heart of the holy land, they could not apply the Word with power to her life. All that time they were unable to use the Word to heal her; adversely, they used the Word to bring judgement on her life! But then comes Jesus . . .

John 5:19:

Jesus gave them this answer: 'Very truly I tell you, the Son can do nothing by himself; he can do only what he sees his Father doing, because whatever the Father does the Son also does.

He comes as the Word of God, sent out 'from the Father, full of grace and truth' (John 1:14).

John 1:17:

> For the law was given through Moses; grace and truth
> came through Jesus Christ.

There is apparently a great difference between the Word
set in stone and the Word that became flesh, the Living
– *rhema* – Word. The Word set in stone had a purpose. It
showed the holiness of God and revealed at the same time
the incompetence of man and the *unattainability* of the
standard that was set. This revealed the need for a Messiah
even more vehemently. Man would never have been able to
gratify or reach the Father in his own strength.

**Through
Jesus a new
reality was
introduced.**

Through Jesus a new reality was
introduced. The One who supplies life and
love opened a living way to the Father.
It was no longer only the high priest who
once a year had careful access to God (the
Father). No, the opposite has become
true! Every child of God now has unlimited
access to the Father and even *in* the Father.
And it goes even further, for the Father makes His home *in*
our hearts. The law and commandments have been fulfilled
and the fulfilled commandments have become promises!

The Great Commandment

And so, the Great Commandment, when Jesus takes it from
the Old Testament and places it in the New Testament,
undergoes a metamorphosis.

Mark 12:29-30:

> 'The most important [commandment],' answered Jesus,
> 'is this: 'Hear, O Israel: The Lord our God, the Lord is

one. Love the Lord your God with all your heart and with all your soul and with all your mind and with all your strength.'

Where it was first an unattainable command, Jesus now says: 'Hear, O Israel, do you know what is coming? The Father will come and make His home in your heart, and you will be able to receive the fullness of His love.' When this happens to you, this commandment will turn into a promise and you will be able to 'Love the Lord your God with all your heart and with all your soul and with all your mind and with all your strength'!

The woman caught in adultery

In John 8 we read the account of another woman. The Pharisees and teachers of the law caught a woman in adultery (by herself?) and brought her to Jesus.

John 8:3-6:

> *The teachers of the law and the Pharisees brought in a woman caught in adultery. They made her stand before the group and said to Jesus, 'Teacher, this woman was caught in the act of adultery. In the Law Moses commanded us to stone such women. Now what do you say?' They were using this question as a trap, in order to have a basis for accusing him. But Jesus bent down and started to write on the ground with his finger.*

The Pharisees and teachers of the law were powerless to change the situation of the bleeding woman, but they were powerful enough to use the Word as a trap for Jesus to bring judgement to a woman.

Love finds its origin not in the law, but in relationship!

What happens when the Pharisees and teachers of the law bring this woman to Jesus? A confrontation takes place between the written Word (the law of Moses) and the Living Word, where grace (and love and forgiveness) have been added to the truth. Love finds its origin not in the law, but in relationship!

The Pharisees and teachers of the law confront Jesus with a question: to pass judgement on this woman according to the law, or to ignore the law. Everyone anxiously awaits Jesus' response, but instead Jesus reaches down and writes with His finger in the sand.

You could ask yourself what Jesus wrote in the sand. Some believe He was writing names, and that is a possibility. But something else stood out to me. The Pharisees and teachers of the law came with the law. The law was given by God to Moses, written on two stone tablets. God had written the Ten Commandments with His finger on the tablets. And now here is Jesus, and He is God. And with His finger in the sand, being God's finger, He 'overwrites' the law with grace and love.

The promise for us too

And now for us! Jesus tells us in Matthew exactly what it's about.

Matthew 5:20:

For I tell you that unless your righteousness surpasses that of the Pharisees and the teachers of the law, you will certainly not enter the kingdom of heaven.

It is important for us to realise that we neither possess the power nor ability to make this happen. And we find ourselves in good company, for Jesus says of Himself: '. . . the Son can do nothing by himself' (John 5:19). No, we can't do it, but in complete dependency on the Father and through the power of the Holy Spirit, it is possible. It is for us a matter of receiving the Father's love while we rest in His arms. Then we will see that we are actually able to fulfil the following scriptures.

Romans 13:8-10:

> *Let no debt remain outstanding, except the continuing debt to love one another, for whoever loves others has fulfilled the law. The commandments, 'You shall not commit adultery,' 'You shall not murder,' 'You shall not steal,' 'You shall not covet,' and whatever other command there may be, are summed up in this one command: 'Love your neighbour as yourself.' Love does no harm to a neighbour. Therefore love is the fulfilment of the law.*

The finger of Jesus in the sand which 'overwrote' the law makes it possible for us to really live. No longer do we live under the law, but in freedom, through the grace that is given to us.

2 Corinthians 3:3,6:

> *You show that you are a letter from Christ, the result of our ministry, written not with ink but with the Spirit of the living God, not on tablets of stone but on tablets of human hearts. He has made us competent as ministers of a new covenant – not of the letter but of the Spirit; for the letter kills, but the Spirit gives life.*

Time to reflect:

I think at this point there is much to reflect on. The most important thing is that you don't take this chapter for mere knowledge, but that you discover what the Father through these words wants to speak to your heart. Sometimes it's a small gesture, a word or a thought, that will encourage you to start on something in your own life. Are you finding it difficult to discover something yourself? Ask the Holy Spirit to reveal something to you, and set time apart, perhaps while you're listening to some restful music (or when you go for a walk in a forest or on the beach).

To listen:

Bart de Krijger, *Circa Divina*

Additional reading:

Jack Frost, *Experiencing Father's Embrace* (Shippensburg, PA: Destiny Image Publishers, 2002)

Space for notes/reflections:

ELEVEN

His holy name

Ezekiel 36:23 (*The Message*):

*Then the nations will realize who I really am,
that I am God, when I show my holiness through
you so that they can see it with their own eyes.*

Revelation from God

I have spoken in this book a lot about who God really is. That
He is a Father, and that He also *wants* to be a Father to us. We
also talked about the identity of sonship. The possibility to
not only be a child *of* God, but to also be a son or a daughter
to Him. In this chapter, we will look at God's plan, how He
is revealing Himself in this time. He has been preparing this
revelation for a long time. After all, Jesus came to earth as a
man to reveal the Father.

John 14:9:

> . . . *Anyone who has seen me has seen the Father...*

Unfortunately, over the years we have lost this image of God.
The Church has largely become religion and institution. In
the Middle Ages, the relationship with the Father was almost
lost completely. But I still believe that all of this was part of
God's plan. As Israel was to enter the promised land by being
dependent on Him, likewise, it was necessary for the Church

to learn that you cannot build the kingdom of God in your own strength. Fred Wright, former director of Partners In Harvest/global, noted that you can see an advancement in history of God revealing to the Church who He really is.[4]

The Reformation

Look at the start of the Reformation in 1517 in Augsburg; this was 500 years ago. In the following chapter I will highlight another side of the Reformation, but here we will focus on how God revealed Himself in that time. For it is in this time that people started to know Jesus again as their personal Saviour. Of course, the Father and the Holy Spirit were present also, but Jesus stood in the 'spotlight', so to speak. Since the Bible had been translated, the Word of God was now available for the first time to the 'layperson'.

In 2016, I was invited to translate Johannes Hartl at Mission Possible in Nijkerk, the Netherlands. It was a privilege to be asked for this. Hartl is the founder of the prayer house in Augsburg. Since 2005, they have ongoing prayer and worship times, twenty-four hours a day, 365 days a year! His desire is that 500 years after the Reformation, a new reconciliation of the churches will take place.

The revelation of Jesus that started 500 years ago is still expressing itself today in extraordinary ways. Hartl: 'A Muslim from Egypt has landed in Germany. Jesus appeared to him in a vision. He has become a Christian and is now looking for a church, because he wants to get baptised. The pastor points out to him that it would be wise to approach things with caution. Perhaps it is better not to be baptised in public, this could result in severe consequences when the

---

4. Fred and Sharon Wright, *The World's Greatest Revivals* (Shippensburg, PA: Destiny Image Publishers, 2007).

family or other Muslims find out. The Egyptian man looks the pastor in the eyes and says: "You have never really seen Jesus, have you?"'

We should be aware that the face of 'our' Church in the near future might drastically change by Muslims coming to the Christian faith through radical conversion.

Azusa Street

From 1906 till 1909 in a Methodist church in Los Angeles, USA, we see the 'Azusa Street Revival' taking place. A new, powerful revelation of the Holy Spirit. Here too, the Father is present, as well as the Son. But this time it's the Holy Spirit who stands in the spotlights.

The Father

Now we get to the nineties where, in many places around the world, people are receiving revelation on the Father heart of God. One of the first who carried this revelation was Jack Winter. Later, he passed his mantle on to James Jordan, who after some time called Fatherheart Ministries into life. This ministry is largely known through the Fatherheart Schools they organise worldwide. Then, John and Carol Arnott became very well known. In 1994 and later, there was an outpouring of the love of the Father in their church in Toronto. Since this time, God the Father has been in the spotlight.

One time it occurred to me that since the Reformation the Church has hardly changed. This surprised me. I thought, why not first renew the Church? Later I understood why this was not possible. We are the Church, and only in dependency on the Father can we really change. Together with help from Jesus and the Holy Spirit can we really begin to live in sonship. For this we first need the revelation of Jesus, the Holy Spirit and the Father. Believers who are transformed in this way will, in their turn, in the times ahead, start to reveal the renewed Church.

The removal

Earlier we talked about the choice Adam and Eve made to be independent. By this choice, it was no longer possible for them to live in sonship. At the same time, they were no longer able to be carriers of the image of God. They had become orphans.

How did the Father respond to this? It was the worst thing that could have happened to Him. He, who had made man the crown of His creation, meant for them to spend eternity with Him. He wanted to love them, and be a Father to them. So, what does He do? He sends them out of the garden. Why? Because by leaving them in the garden there was a possibility (if they ate from the Tree of Life) they would stay orphans forever.

However, from the beginning, the Father had a plan for restoration. We often think this has to do with our own restoration, but it's bigger than that. It is, of course, important that we come out from 'orphanness' into sonship, but this is not God's final goal. It is the means by which to reach the final goal. Not us, but He, will be central. The same goes for conversion (or new birth). Conversion is not the end goal, but the *means* by which we are able to reach our end goal: coming home to the arms of the Father!

[Our goal is:] coming home to the arms of the Father!

The announcement of the restoration

Ezekiel 36 contains one of the most beautiful announcements of the restoration God has in mind. Naturally, this first concerns Israel, I don't want to steal away from that. But through the promise God made to Abraham, we are now also benefactors of that promise. We read this in the letter to the Galatians.

Galatians 3:7-8:

Understand, then, that those who have faith are children of Abraham. Scripture foresaw that God would justify the Gentiles by faith, and announced the gospel in advance to Abraham: 'All nations will be blessed through you.'

But in the prophetic word God speaks in Ezekiel 36, He begins in a somewhat curious way. He compares Israel's walk to the monthly uncleanness of a woman.

Ezekiel 36:16-17:

*Again the word of the Lord came to me: 'Son of man, when the people of Israel were living in their own land, they defiled it by their conduct and their actions. **Their conduct was like a woman's monthly uncleanness in my sight.***

We 'coincidentally' talked about this in the previous chapter. Why does God use this specific example for Israel? Why didn't He simply say: 'Israel, you made mistakes!' He did not, He spoke of monthly uncleanness ...

The first part of the verse is about the defilement of the land. In the previous chapter, we read in Leviticus that a woman's monthly uncleanness is transferable. In other words, God is showing Israel, through a clear example, how her behaviour affects the land. But it goes even further, for God chose Israel to be His people. Because of her behaviour, He takes this example of the monthly uncleanness. Why? To show that while they are in this state, it is impossible for Him to have an intimate relationship with the people of Israel.

But there is more. God shows that there is more at play than just the defilement of the land. This is something that personally and deeply touches Him. He says He dispersed them among the nations, yet they continued in their ways. And by this, they, as the carriers of His Name, have profaned His Name.

Ezekiel 36:19-21:

> *I dispersed them among the nations, and they were scattered through the countries; I judged them according to their conduct and their actions. And wherever they went among the nations they profaned my holy name, for it was said of them, 'These are the Lord's people, and yet they had to leave his land.' I had concern for my holy name, which the people of Israel profaned among the nations where they had gone.*

This is so important to God, that in verses 20-24 of Ezekiel 36, He mentions five times (!) that they defiled His Holy Name. When God repeats something just once, we already know He is trying to communicate something important to us. How important is it then, when He repeats something five times! I don't really know any other scriptures where this happens. Why is this such an important issue to God? I think that when something is important to Him, it's also important for us to understand. God is working at His plan of restoration. From the beginning, he purposed mankind to be the carriers of His image.

Genesis 1:26:

> Let us make mankind in our image, in our likeness . . .

Name carriers

Because we are family, we are also name carriers. A name is very important. A name describes the essence of a person. Anneke and I have eight children. It has not always been easy for all eight of them. Some of them had a certain 'name' at school. When their brother or

> **Because we are family, we are also name carriers.**

sister would start new at school, some would say to them: 'Oh, you're one of the Bruggemans, are you?' This had in itself nothing to do with me, for I wasn't in their class, I had never even been a student at their school. Yet my name was being used, and not in a good way. They had formed an image with the name 'Bruggeman'. How did this happen? Because my children carry my name.

Returning to God and His plan

From the beginning, God desired to be Father and to be known as Father. Through the Fall, His children are growing up as orphans on the earth. This hurts Him. It is difficult for man to know God well, because He is Spirit and we are flesh. Paul describes this in his first letter to the Corinthians.

1 Corinthians 2:14:

> The person without the Spirit does not accept the things that come from the Spirit of God but considers them

foolishness, and cannot understand them because they are discerned only through the Spirit.

For this reason, He chose the people of Israel, to whom He could be a Father again. It was far from an ideal situation, for through sin He was unable to be one with them. But under specific circumstances He was able to live among them. They would then also carry His Name, and so God was able to be seen on earth, through His people. This way the other peoples of the earth would see through them the image of who God really is. At least, that was the plan.

In Ezekiel, we see things vehemently going wrong. It appeared Israel was not capable of representing God in a right way. The 'not-knowing' Him for who He really is does hurt Him, but instead of measuring out punishment, He approaches the situation differently. He basically says that we need to see this as a learning curve: 'You can't do it!' Or better said: 'You can't do it without Me.'

This might sound familiar to some of us. The simple fact is, there are things in your life that will go completely wrong. They just will not work. Instead of trying to keep on going and hitting the wall over and over again, you can also say to God: 'I can't do it, I need you. Can I be dependent on You?' Do you know how much a good father loves it, when his (somewhat older) children come to him and tell him they still need him?

(Time to reflect)

God initiates

God says to Ezekiel: 'Go and tell them. I will take over. I will make sure that My Name will be purified. For what reason?

Because I want to be known by those who don't know Me, or have a wrong image of Me, for who I really am.'

Ezekiel 36:22-23:

*Therefore say to the Israelites, 'This is what the Sovereign Lord says: **it is not for your sake, people of Israel, that I am going to do these things, but for the sake of my holy name, which you have profaned among the nations where you have gone. I will show the holiness** of my great name, which has been profaned among the nations, the name you have profaned among them. Then the nations will know that I am the Lord, declares the Sovereign Lord, when I am proved holy through you before their eyes.*

This scripture is worded so powerfully in *The Message* translation by Petersen, that I will also add it here:

Therefore, tell Israel, 'Message of God, the Master: I'm not doing this for you, Israel. I'm doing it for me, to save my character, my holy name, which you've blackened in every country where you've gone. I'm going to put my great and holy name on display, the name that has been ruined in so many countries, the name that you blackened wherever you went. Then the nations will realize who I really am, that I am God, when I show my holiness through you so that they can see it with their own eyes.

We need to be aware of the way God starts here: 'You have defiled the land, you have blackened My Name, you have profaned My Name.' His answer, His solution to the problem, is this: 'I have a plan. I know of a remedy for your unholiness. The solution is that I am holy. The only way you can become holy, or better said, can carry My holiness, is when I fill you with My holiness! But to be able to carry My holiness, some changes need to happen inside of you. But don't worry, I will take care of that too!'

> **The only way you can ... carry My holiness, is when I fill you with My holiness!**

Ezekiel 36:24-29:

> *For I will take you out of the nations; I will gather you from all the countries and bring you back into your own land. I will sprinkle clean water on you, and you will be clean; I will cleanse you from all your impurities and from all your idols. **I will give you a new heart and put a new spirit in you; I will remove from you your heart of stone and give you a heart of flesh. And I will put my Spirit in you and move you to follow my decrees and be careful to keep my laws**. Then you will live in the land I gave your ancestors; you will be my people, and I will be your God. I will save you from all your uncleanness.*

This is what the world has been waiting for! Paul speaks of this in his letter to the Romans.

Romans 8:19:

> *For the creation waits in eager expectation for the children of God to be **revealed**.*

The world is not waiting for the sons of God, but the *revealing* of the sons of God! And this will happen the moment we start living in sonship. Then will He, through His people, be known for who He truly is! Just like Jesus, who says:

John 14:9:

Anyone who has seen me has seen the Father.

His holy Name

It's wonderful to read and realise that this is something we also can be a part of. But something else has come to my attention at the reading of the scriptures. Very often we read 'for his name's sake'. I always took this line for a simple addition, nothing special. But when this dawned on me, I suddenly realised its incredible significance.

I will give a few examples, but you can, of course, find many more yourself.

Psalm 23:3:

he refreshes my soul. He guides me along the right paths ***for his name's sake***.

What it says here is that the refreshing of my soul and His guiding me along the right paths is firstly not about me. I am the means by which God achieves His goal, which is: to make me a worthy carrier of His name.

Psalm 106:8:

*Yet he saved them **for his name's sake**, to make his mighty power known.*

Also in this psalm He reveals that salvation serves a higher purpose than just salvation by itself. Through salvation, the people of which the psalmist speaks have come into a position of liberty to make His power known, so that God can be seen for who He truly is.

1 John 2:12:

> I am writing to you, dear children, because your sins have been forgiven **on account of his name.**

In 1 John, we get an example from the New Testament. This has given me a totally different perspective on the reason why my sins have been forgiven. I have always put myself at the centre. I need forgiveness for my sins, so that I can be cleansed and I can get to heaven, etc. What it says here, though, is that I am not the goal, but that I am a means by which God reaches His goal. This goal is not that I look holy, but that He can reveal who He is through me!

Psalm 25:11:

> **For the sake of your name,** Lord, forgive my iniquity, though it is great.

Again, now in the Psalms, it is pointed out why God should forgive me my iniquities. For the sake of His Name!

The same is true for the forgiveness of sins of which John writes. We are not at the centre of things. It is no longer about my – or about *our* – ministry! That is mostly irrelevant. Being well-equipped can actually hinder us, because it's not about our 'ability'. Everything is focused on Him and making His Name great.

John 17:26:

> *I have made you known to them, and will continue to make you known in order that the love you have for me may be in them and that I myself may be in them.*

This is what Jesus says, what He believes in; He will continue to make known the Name of His Father.

Our Father

But I have saved the best for last. We all know, of course, the prayer: 'Our Father'. It is the prayer that Jesus taught us to pray. After everything we just learned, it is very intriguing that the most important prayer of all starts with: 'hallowed be your name …'

Matthew 6:9-10:

> *This, then, is how you should pray: 'Our Father in heaven, hallowed be your name, your kingdom come, your will be done, on earth as it is in heaven.*

When I read this in *The Message* translation, I was even more surprised:

> *Our Father in heaven,* **Reveal who you are.**

Wonderful! This is now our prayer, and it's in total harmony with the desire that resides in the heart of the Father. And at the same time, we are in fact also saying: 'Father, reveal who You are, so that it may be revealed who we are.'

Our Father in heaven, Reveal who you are *(The Message)*

One name carrier

I haven't yet forgotten what I started with. I am well aware that the prophetic word in Ezekiel was first spoken to Israel. And this word is very relevant today! My desire is that the verses in which Paul speaks on this topic, in his letter to the Ephesians, will in our day come to fruition more than ever before.

Ephesians 2:13-16:

But now in Christ Jesus you who once were far away have been brought near by the blood of Christ. For he himself is our peace, who has made the two groups one and has destroyed the barrier, the dividing wall of hostility, by setting aside in his flesh the law with its commands and regulations. His purpose was to create in himself one new humanity out of the two, thus making peace, and in one body to reconcile both of them to God through the cross, by which he put to death their hostility.

Ephesians 2:14-15 (*The Message*):

Then he started over. Instead of continuing with two groups of people separated by centuries of animosity and suspicion, he created a new kind of human being, a fresh start for everybody.

In the next chapter I will expound further on the role Israel has today.

Time to reflect:

I have one more question I want to ask. Why does God always want to be nice to us? Even when time after time we mess things up? We now know, of course, that it is for His holy

Name's sake. But is there more to consider? Perhaps it's a good idea to list all the things He does for us.

- Without us asking for it, we see that the Father **blesses** us!

Genesis 1:27-28:

*So God created mankind in his own image, in the image of God he created them; male and female he created them. 28 God **blessed** them . . .*

But He does even more for us:

- It was God's idea to provide us a **helper**.

Genesis 2:18:

*The Lord God said, 'It is not good for the man to be alone. I will make **a helper** suitable for him.'*

Denise Jordan explains in her book *The Forgotten Feminine*[5] that the word 'helper' in the Bible is often used in relation to God. We can derive from this that the helper God gave to Adam was meant to help him in a similar way as God wants to help us. She is, so to speak, the 'Bride of the Garden'.

- He gives us a **new heart** and a **new spirit** (Ezekiel 36).
- He puts His **Spirit** in us and even **causes us to walk in His ways** (Ezekiel 36).
- He gives us the same **glory** He also gave to Jesus.

---

5. Denise Jordan, *The Forgotten Feminine* (The National Library of New Zealand, 2014).

John 17:22:

*I have given them the **glory** that you gave me, that they may be one as we are one –*

- He gives us the same **love** He also gave to Jesus.

John 17:23:

. . . that you sent me and have loved them even as you have loved me.

- He prepares **good** works for us.

Ephesians 2:10:

For we are God's handiwork, created in Christ Jesus to do good works, which God prepared in advance for us to do.

- He gives us **redemption, grace** and **forgiveness**.

Ephesians 1:7:

*In him we have **redemption** through his blood, the **forgiveness** of sins, in accordance with the riches of God's **grace.***

- He gives us **righteous acts**.

Revelation 19:6b-8:

Hallelujah! For our Lord God Almighty reigns. Let us rejoice and be glad and give him glory! For the wedding of the Lamb has come, and his bride has made herself ready. Fine linen, bright and clean, was given her to wear.' (Fine linen stands for the **righteous acts of God's holy people**.)

Why would God the Father go through all this trouble, what is His final purpose and desire? After His ascension, when Jesus arrived in heaven, the Father made Him a promise. He most likely thanked Him that He had given everything, that His work had been completed. Then the Father said: 'Go and sit at My right hand; now it is My turn. I will make your enemies a footstool for your feet' Freely translated, of course.

Luke 20:42-43:

> The Lord said to my Lord: 'Sit at my right hand until I make your enemies a footstool for your feet.'

There is another thing the Father probably said to Jesus. I think He said to His son, the second Adam: 'It is not good You are alone. I will make a helper (Bride) suitable for You.' The Bride of the new city, the New Jerusalem.

It is not good You are alone. I will make a helper (Bride) suitable for You.

And He wants the Son to have the most beautiful bride there ever was, and therefore He gives us everything and says: 'I am Papa, and I will make it happen!'

To listen:

Ruth Fazal, 'Let the Bride See'

Additional reading:

Denise Jordan, *The Forgotten Feminine* (Wellington, NZ: The National Library of New Zealand, 2014)

Fred and Sharon Wright, *The World's Greatest Revivals* (Shippensburg, PA: Destiny Image Publishers, 2007)

Website:

PIH, www.partnersinharvest.org

Space for notes/reflections:

TWELVE

The Father, The Son and Israel

Exodus 4:22 (*The Message*):

*Then you are to tell Pharaoh, 'God's Message:
Israel is my son, my firstborn! I told you,
"Free my son so that he can serve me."'*

Our journey to Israel

One time we travelled with a group of people to Israel during Yom Kippur, and the Feast of Tabernacles. On our travels, together with hundreds of other people, we witnessed a blood-moon on the Mount of Olives. During our ten day stay, we visited many places. We wandered around in the Old City and stopped at the Wailing Wall. Unfortunately, we were just out of time to do a virtual walk through the Third Temple at the Temple Institute. We visited Bethel, where Jacob had a dream and where God confirmed to Jacob the promise He had given to Abraham. We also went to Shiloh, where the Ark of the Covenant stood.

The older brother

Jeanette Geelhoed lives and works in Israel and she told us many things about the land. This enriched us greatly. It was also wonderful to have an afternoon to talk with Ruth Fazal, a musician living in Jerusalem, about all sorts of things. At one point, Ruth asked me why I had come to Israel. When I considered this, I realised my motivation had changed. Before I left, I thought it would be a great idea during this trip to forge new relations, to make new connections, so that later I would be able to organise something to bring the Father heart to Israel. But during this trip something had changed. I had come to Israel, seeing it as my 'older brother'. With the several orthodox Jews I met there, I tasted an intimacy with God and a deep desire to do His will, that I greatly envy. And so, my answer to Ruth was: 'I think I want to sit at the feet of my older brother and want to listen to what he can tell me of God the Father.'

The artwork

Shortly after, I experienced something I will never forget. Driving from Jerusalem along the Dead Sea we arrived in Arad, to visit an artwork called the 'Fountain of Tears'. Arad is a place in Israel, twenty-five kilometres west of the Dead Sea and forty-five kilometres east of Beersheba. It lies at the edge of the desert of Judah, north-east of the Negev, not far from Masada and about 640 metres above sea level. Here lives artist Rick Wienecke. Fascinated by the State of Israel, raised from the ashes of the Holocaust, there arose in him a desire to be a part of it. As if by a miracle, this Canadian was granted a permanent visa to Israel and has since lived there for more than thirty years.

In 2001 God spoke to Rick about the design of an artwork. It had to portray a dialogue between the crucified Christ and the Holocaust! For Rick this was at first an unspeakable thing. He saw no possible way of portraying these two highly sensitive matters, and in Israel of all places. But God won and Rick began.

When we entered the space where Rick built the 'Fountain of Tears', my mouth fell wide open and I gasped for breath. The building has a sheet acting as a ceiling and a warm yellow light falls on the wall. I saw a wall, built up with great white 'Jerusalem stones'. The wall was divided into seven parts, separated by six pillars of natural stone, having water slowly running down them from a spring above. Out of the wall, as it were, emerges in part the crucified Christ; seven times, depicting the seven words of Jesus on the cross. The six pillars symbolise the 6 million Jews who died in the Holocaust. There was no cross, but there was the crucified One. The water slowly dripped down the pillars represented the tears that are spoken of in the book of Jeremiah.

Jeremiah 9:1:

Oh, that my head were a spring of water and my eyes a fountain of tears! I would weep day and night for the slain of my people.

The Message:

I wish my head were a well of water and my eyes fountains of tears. So I could weep day and night for casualties among my dear, dear people.

The water then runs down under the floor to the front of the building, where six olive trees stand, being watered by this.

The suffering

In front of each one of the seven images of the crucified Christ is a life-size bronze-made figure, a survivor of the Holocaust. Through the different stances they take, each figure portrays a poignant expression of one of the words of

Christ on the cross. So is there the expression of the word of the cross where Jesus cried out: *'Eloi, Eloi, lema sabachthani'*, meaning: 'My God, my God, why have you forsaken me?' Documentation has revealed that hundreds or thousands of Jews, the moment they entered the gas chambers, cried out Psalm 22:1: 'My God, my God, why have you forsaken me?'

In these images, Jesus, as well as the figures of the Holocaust survivors, has a shaved head. Jesus even has a number on His left arm, just like every prisoner of the concentration camps. This was especially difficult for Rick to do, but because God kept insisting, he went through with it. He chose the number 1534, for 1 + 5 = 6, which stands for the 6 million Jews that died. And 3 + 4 = 7, the seven words of Jesus on the cross.

When the artwork was finished and the visitors came, someone asked if the number had yet another meaning. It is in fact in Mark 15:34 where Jesus utters the words: *'Eloi, Eloi, lema sabachthani* . . . My God, my God, why have you forsaken me?' Another time someone ask if the 1 could also be interpreted as the capital letter 'I'. In the English language, there is only one Bible book that begins with the letter 'I' which is Isaiah. In that case, the number would refer to Isaiah 53:4, which says:

> **My God, my God, why have you forsaken me?**

Isaiah 53:4:

Surely he took up our pain and bore our suffering, yet we considered him punished by God, stricken by him, and afflicted.

It seems God wants to tell us that the suffering of His people in the Holocaust is connected to the suffering of His Son. We know that the suffering of Christ is for us literally of vital importance. What is the benefit of the suffering of the Jewish people? For them, and for us? I ask this question, for I do not have a clear answer at this time. I do believe that in the times ahead, we will get more insight into the matters of suffering and obedience.

Israel

We have often seen Israel as one who has yet to convert. Moreover, how many Christians raise themselves above Israel, demanding its place and are now saying that they themselves are the 'spiritual Israel'? Despite the fact that I do not support this theology, I must confess that after my trip to Israel, I started seeing things I have not seen before. I saw myself and the church I belong to in a position that Jews could only come into if they accepted Christ. And that is something I do not believe anymore . . . I will try to take you to the place where the change in my thinking happened.

Romans 11:11:

> *Again I ask: did they stumble so as to fall beyond recovery? Not at all! Rather, because of their transgression, salvation has come to the Gentiles* **to make Israel envious***.*

This has always been the verse that motivated me to think it was the job of Christians to bring the Jews to repentance. I have always nonchalantly thought, being aware of it or not, that the Jews will only really be relevant again when they have accepted Christ. But what is God the Father's plan with His people?

Romans 11:8:

> as it is written: **'God gave them a spirit of stupor, eyes that could not see and ears that could not hear, to this very day.'**

Could it be that the change we are waiting for is not dependent on our zeal to convert them, but on the moment when God Himself removes the veil which He has pulled over the eyes His people?

> **Could it be that the change we are waiting for is not dependent on our zeal to convert them, but on the moment when God Himself removes the veil which He has pulled over the eyes of His people?**

We have to ask ourselves if we, as Christians, have shown something in the last 2,000 years that would have provoked the Jewish people to jealousy. I fear that throughout history we have mostly achieved the opposite. Not only have the crusades horribly contributed to this, but also the pride with which we have approached them, has led more to hostility rather than jealousy.

Since the Reformation, Jesus has again come 'into view' as our personal Saviour. In 1517 Martin Luther nailed his 95 theses on the door of the castle church in Wittenberg, but this new light also has a dark side. This great reformer is, strangely enough, the one who later opened the way for Hitler's persecution of the Jews! At the end of his life, Luther increasingly emphasised anti-Jewish stereotypes. A few centuries later, this view gave rise to the theology that opened the door to the Holocaust.

THE FATHER, THE SON AND ISRAEL

Luther-researcher René Süss comments on this: 'The perpetrators weren't devils, but people who adopted Luther's demonising of the Jews and combined it with racism. There is evidence of some cases where after a reading of Luther, people would severely start persecuting Jews. Evidently Luther's Christian anti-Semitism greatly influenced the climate of Europe. Accordingly, Hitler's political testament greatly resembles the theological testament of Luther, who Hitler admired and with whom he shared the common desire for a "Judenreine" world.'[6]

The wall is destroyed

Certainly, in the letter to the Ephesians there is mentioned that the wall of hostility is destroyed. The question is, how are we supposed to interpret this? For it seems that in past centuries, Christianity has caused more hostility than unity.

Ephesians 2:14-18:

For he himself is our peace, who has made the two groups one and has destroyed the barrier, the dividing wall of hostility, by setting aside in his flesh the law with its commands and regulations. His purpose was to create in himself one new humanity out of the two, thus making peace, and in one body to reconcile both of them to God through the cross, by which he put to death their hostility. He came and preached peace to you who were far away and peace to those who were near. For through him we both have access to the Father by one Spirit.

This is talking about the *Mcz Jitsa*, the wall that was built around the temple. Historian Josephus Flavius records that

---

6. Quote taken from Edo Sturm, in the daily newspaper *Trouw* (Netherlands), 6 November 2005.

in those days there was a sign on the wall above the entrance to the Outer Courts. On this sign was written: 'Forbidden for non-Jews, on penalty of stoning.' Paul tells us in this part of the letter to the Ephesians that the wall was effectively destroyed. This was, for the people in those days, a shock to hear! Just like the tearing of the temple veil was an enormous shock. Paul explains: 'He came and preached peace to you who were far away and peace to those who were near' (Ephesians 2:17).

Relationship instead of religion

We see that in a way, God was only the God of the Jews. He had told to them precisely what the customary rules were. The temple was the dwelling place of God. The moment Jesus dies, He tells us that the temple will be destroyed inside and out, as it were. This is the start of a new relationship that God the Father wants to enjoy with *all* His children.

> **This is the start of a new relationship that God the Father wants to enjoy with *all* His children.**

God has already met the requirements of the New Covenant from His side. He says: 'I am ready to replace religion with relationship.' Aside from this renewal, by which the heathen can also come into relationship with the Father, the fact is that God has caused the Jewish people to fall into a deep sleep, causing them to not (yet) be able to walk in this truth. Seeing as God caused them to fall asleep, it should be obvious to us that it's not our job to wake them up. The Father will, in His plan, in the right timing, open their eyes and ears again. He will wake them up!

For us remains the question of how we should position ourselves in the meantime. What is the relationship between us and the Jewish people? First it is important that we find information about God's plan with us and His plan with Israel.

A hardening in part

The following scriptures in Romans 11 give us a very important fact.

Romans 11:25-26:

> I do not want you to be ignorant of this mystery, brothers and sisters, so that you may not be conceited: **Israel has experienced a hardening in part until the full number of the Gentiles has come in, and in this way all Israel will be saved.**

What a wonderful promise God makes here to His people! All Israel will be saved. If there was but one nation that would have a right to this, it would be Israel. What suffering has this nation endured throughout history! But their suffering will lead to the greatest victory. Just like the suffering of Jesus produced the greatest victory.

Could it be possible that the Father has pulled a veil over our eyes too? A covering through which we cannot clearly see the place of God's people. And could it be that in these days, through the revelation of His Father's heart for us, we will now discover His great and unconditional love for Israel and the Jewish people, as well as their role in the end times?

Hyacinth Bos-Halfhide, writer of the book *Waarom Israël? (Why Israel?)* writes in her foreword: 'A few years ago I specifically asked God the Father what His desire was. I said to Him: "Father, I always come to you with my wish-list, but what's on Your wish-list?" He answered one word: *Israel*.'[7]

Everything indicates that our position is shifting from a Church that is independently working for God, to a Church in a place of total dependency on God the Father. In this place, we can discover and experience intimacy with the Father. Right here, in the heart of the Father, we will discover the mystery of the place of the Jewish people and His passionate love for them.

> **'Father, I always come to you with my wish-list, but what's on Your wish-list?' He answered in one word: Israel.**

The truth

How does the Father look at His people at the moment? Our Greek way of thinking and our Protestant-inspired prayers have told us that there is only one truth. So, the moment we think we're in the truth, and someone else is acting or behaving differently, we assume that they are not walking in the truth. Thinking from such a mindset and then applying it to the case of the Jewish people, we have tried to convince them of their error and convert them to what we see as the only truth.

The Hebrew way of thinking, however, is very different. I would like to demonstrate this by using a well-known example in which two blind people are asked to give a description of an elephant. The first blind person is being led to the back of an elephant and he starts to describe it: 'An elephant has two large surfaces and in the middle is some

---

7. https://hyacinth-hosea.com/.

kind of cord which turns fuzzy at the end.' The second blind person is taken to the front of the elephant and describes the elephant as follows: 'He has in the middle some kind of vacuum cleaner hose, and on both sides, hard curved horns and also on each side some sort of large leather flaps.' Both descriptions of the elephant are correct, despite them being totally different. So very different, yet both form *together* one truth.

We have formed an image of Israel and define our mutual relationship on the basis of *our* thinking. Let us see if we can discover how God the Father looks at Israel.

Exodus 4:22-23:

> Then say to Pharaoh, 'This is what the Lord says: **Israel is my firstborn son,** and I told you, "Let my son go, **so that he may worship me**." But you refused to let him go; so I will kill your firstborn son.'

This is, of course, in the Old Testament. But if we read carefully, we see that it does not say that Israel is *like* a firstborn son of God the Father, but that Israel *is* His firstborn son! The following verse is taken from the book of Isaiah.

Isaiah 49:15-16:

> Can a mother forget the baby at her breast and have no compassion on the child she has borne? Though she may forget, I will not forget you! See, I have engraved you on the palms of my hands; your walls are ever before me.

Paul writes in his letter to the Romans:

Romans 11:29-32:

> for God's gifts and his call are irrevocable. Just as you who were at one time disobedient to God have now received mercy as a result of their disobedience, so they too have now become disobedient in order that they too may now receive mercy as a result of God's mercy to you. **For God has bound everyone over to disobedience so that he may have mercy on them all.**

Has God for the sake of His great love for us not only given Jesus – but also His 'son' Israel – for us? And if so, what else is there in store for us? What does this mean for our relationship with Israel? I think God is in these times releasing more revelation about this subject than ever before.

Romans 11:11-15:

> Again I ask: did they stumble so as to fall beyond recovery? Not at all! Rather, **because of their transgression, salvation has come to the Gentiles** to make Israel envious. But if their transgression means riches for the world, and their loss means riches for the Gentiles, how much greater riches will their full inclusion bring! I am talking to you Gentiles. Inasmuch as I am the apostle to the Gentiles, I take pride in my ministry in the hope that I may somehow arouse my own people to envy and save some of them. **For if their rejection brought reconciliation to the world, what will their acceptance be but life from the dead?**

Could it be that Israel is still part of God's plan for the entire world, and that even still – through suffering – it occupies a place designated by God? It is quite extraordinary to see that God does not let His love and care for the Jewish people depend on their conversion to Christ. Isaiah prophesies that He will give them back the land for them to occupy.

Isaiah 14:1:

> The Lord will have compassion on Jacob; once again **he will choose Israel and will settle them in their own land.** Foreigners will join them and unite with the descendants of Jacob.

Isaiah 66:8:

> Who has ever heard of such things? Who has ever seen things like this? **Can a country be born in a day or a nation be brought forth in a moment?** Yet no sooner is Zion in labour than she gives birth to her children.

In Romans 11 are some verses that seem to contradict verses from the letter to the Ephesians.

Romans 11:27-28:

> And this is my covenant with them **when I take away their sins.**' As far as the gospel is concerned, they are enemies for your sake; but as far as **election** is concerned, **they are loved on account of the patriarchs** ...

I believe that the destroying of the wall of hostility in these days is entering a new phase. In the times ahead, the promise given to Abraham back in Genesis will come to full fruition, and Israel will be a blessing to all the nations of the earth.

Genesis 26:3-5:

> *Stay in this land for a while, and **I will be with you and will bless you**. For to you and your descendants I will give all these lands and will confirm the oath I swore to your father Abraham. I will make your descendants as numerous as the stars in the sky and will give them all these lands, **and through your offspring all nations on earth will be blessed, because Abraham obeyed me and did everything I required of him,** keeping my commands, my decrees and my instructions.*

This is also spoken of in the New Testament by Paul in the letter to the Galatians.

Galatians 3:8:

> *Scripture foresaw that God would justify the Gentiles by faith, and announced the gospel in advance to Abraham: 'All nations will be blessed through you.'*

Do you remember the story of Job? He lost everything. God told Satan that he could do anything, except take his life. God appears to be doing the same to Israel by letting his beloved son go through the suffering, for the only reason of being victorious at the end. For Satan is not allowed to take from them eternal life. They will forever and always be with Him, and this is currently a mystery to many, what the outworking of the suffering of this people will be to the world.

Hebrews 2:10:

> *In bringing many sons and daughters to glory, it was fitting that God, for whom and through whom everything*

exists, should make the pioneer of their salvation perfect through what he suffered.

For we already know that the promise resting on Abraham and his descendants is yet to come to full fruition. If it happens in our time or in the Millennium of Peace, who can say?

Two become one

I believe with all my heart that the time will come that we will walk in the reality of Ephesians 2:14-18. Eventually a new humanity will come forth. The hostility between the older and the younger brother will forever pass away. Not because we at some point will have done enough or given our best attempt, but because the Father will have taken away both of our veils! We are to turn to Him, for in a total dependency on Him will the restoration take place.

All honour belongs to Him!

Time to reflect:

Of course, I understand it is impossible to cover this subject in one chapter. That was never my intention. I do hope this chapter gives you plenty to reflect on. What is your relationship with Israel, your older brother?

To listen:

Ruth Fazal, CDs *Hineni (Here I Am)* and *So Close* (both are sung in Hebrew) (https://ruthfazal.com/)

To watch:

Ruth Fazal, DVD: *Between Heaven and Earth* (https://ruthfazal.com/)

Rick Wienecke, DVD: *Fountain of Tears* (YouTube: https://youtu.be/UrZzZwYhoTI)

Additional reading:

Hyacinth Halfhide, 'Waarom Israël?' (Why Israel?) (https://hyacinth-hosea.com/)

Website:

Nati Rom, founder Lev HaOlam, www.levhaolam.com

Space for notes/reflections: